Handlettering for

DECORATIVE ARTISTS

Jackie O'Keefe

NORTH LIGHT BOOKS
CINCINNATI, OHIO

DEDICATION

I believe that we are given certain gifts, and it is our responsibility to nurture and develop those gifts and then to pass them on. This book is dedicated to my family and all the students and fellow painters who have encouraged me to "keep on painting" so that I can pass my gift on. Thank you for your continued support and love—especially you, Honey!

02 01 00 99 98   5 4 3 2 1

Library of Congress Cataloging-in-Publication Data

O'Keefe, Jacquelyn
    Handlettering for decorative artists / by Jacquelyn D.
O'Keefe—1st ed.
        p.   cm.
    Includes index.
    ISBN 0-89134-825-5 (pbk.: alk. paper)
    1. Lettering—Technique. I. Title.
NK3600.043 1998
745.6'1—dc21   98-13041
                                         CIP

Edited by Jennifer Long
Production Edited by Michelle Kramer
Interior and cover designed by Candace Haught
Interior photography by John Murphy, Beth O'Keefe
and Greg Albert
Cover illustration by Jackie O'Keefe
Cover photography by John Murphy

ABOUT THE AUTHOR

Jackie O'Keefe has been a decorative painting teacher, designer and author for ten years. She has taught at nine Society of Decorative Painters annual conventions, as well as at miniconventions, at individual chapters of the society and in shops nationwide. She has over two hundred copyrighted designs in pattern packet form and has authored three books of decorative painting projects for Viking Folk Art Publications. She has also written articles for most of the leading magazines currently available to decorative painters.

Jackie's fine art training in college, coupled with many years of intensive study with recognized decorative painting teachers, laid a firm foundation for a diversity of skills in her field. A fascination with embellished lettering and an appreciation of calligraphy led her to implement turn-of-the-century advertising into her designs. Jackie's unique interpretation of letterforms has gained her a reputation as an authority in this combination of graphic and decorative art.

Jackie spends most of her time travel-teaching decorative painting and working on new designs for publication. Her free time activities include reading, silk ribbon embroidery and taking classes in watercolor painting. A love of antiques and Old Colony pink depression glass keeps her and her husband, Pat, rummaging through antique and collectible shops wherever they travel. Jackie and her husband have been married for forty-three years and reside in Merritt Island, Florida. They have six children and fourteen grandchildren.

For information on any of the designs in this book, please write to Jackie at 1290 St. George Road, Merritt Island, Florida 32952, or call her at (407) 452-4100.

CONTENTS

- Gathering Your Supplies

- Starting With Basic Fonts

- Using Your Own Handwriting

- Laying Out Your Design

- Transferring and Painting Lettering

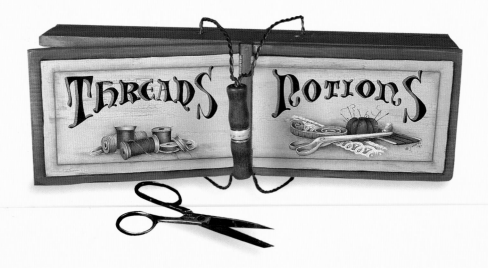

CONTENTS

INTRODUCTION

Quite a few years ago I decided I would like to open a craft shop. My children were growing up, I was tired of being a stay-at-home mom and I had this inner creative drive that needed to be unleashed. I knew I would have to do most of the teaching at the shop in the beginning, so I started taking some classes in areas that I was not proficient. The first classes were in silk flower arranging. When I had filled my home—and everyone else's—I moved on to classes in calligraphy. I really loved working with the lettering and probably spent a bit too much time learning how to write beautifully. But you can only have so many documents and copies of poetry hanging on your walls, so I started working with embellishing letters and adding little flowers and sketches around the sides or at the bottom. The more I learned, the more fascinated I became.

Next, I took a beginner's class in decorative painting. I was hooked. That was the end of the idea of opening a craft shop, but my fascination with lettering never faded. I was often drawn to designs with lettering in them. When I started creating my own designs, I found a perfect outlet for combining my love of calligraphy with my decorative painting.

In this book I would like to share with you what I have learned over the years about using lettering in design and perhaps inspire you to add some personalization or embellishment to your work.

Accuracy lines—Lines that are drawn to act as guidelines for painting so all letters are the same height and on the same plane.

Alphabet—All the letters of a particular font, usually from *A* to *Z*.

Ascenders—Parts of lowercase letters that extend above the line, as with the letters *b* and *l*.

Base coat—The first layer of paint applied to a surface.

Colorbook painting—Basecoating an object with a solid coat of color, filling in from line to line as with a child's coloring book.

Complementary color—The color directly opposite another color on the color wheel.

Condensed letters—Letters that have been elongated, or stretched, to make them taller to fit in narrower spaces.

Connector lines—The lines that connect the main legs of the letters.

Crosshatching—Decorative lines that cross each other at a 90 degree angle.

Dampen—Adding clean water to the painting surface prior to painting to facilitate the flow of paint.

Illumination

Descenders

Embellishments

Deepen or darken—Adding another layer of paint to a painted surface to enrich the color.

Descenders—Parts of lowercase letters that extend below the line, as with the letters *g* and *y*.

Embellishments—Objects added to letters to make them more interesting or decorative.

Extended letters—Letters that have been expanded horizontally to make them wider.

Ferrule—The metal part of a brush that holds the bristles to the handle.

Fleshing out—Adding extra width to letters for beauty and ease of painting.

Float—Using a sideloaded brush to paint on shadows or highlights.

Font—The name printers use to distinguish one alphabet form from another.

Furbelow—A Victorian term for fussy, busy trim added to clothing or furniture.

Highlights—Light areas in the object, usually where light is reflected or shines.

Illumination—Adding extra details around a capital letter to make it more decorative or noticeable.

Italic—Letters that slant to one side.

GLOSSARY

Legs—Basic lines that make up a letter; not the crossbars.

Majuscules—Uppercase or capital letters.

Manuscript fonts—Fonts that were developed and written before the printing press came into use.

Mechanical spacing—Distance between letters that is measured with a ruler.

Miniscules—Lowercase or uncapitalized letters.

Monochromatic colors—Colors that are all of the same hue, such as sky blue, midnight blue, turquoise-blue and gray-blue.

Negative space—The area of a design that has nothing in it.

Neutralized color—A color that has been mixed with a touch of its complement or an earth tone to make it grayer or not as bright.

Notches—Small, pointed projections on the side of the legs of letters.

Optical spacing—Distance between letters that is pleasing to the eye.

Pale wash—Paint thinned down with water or medium to create a pale, transparent color.

Monochromatic colors

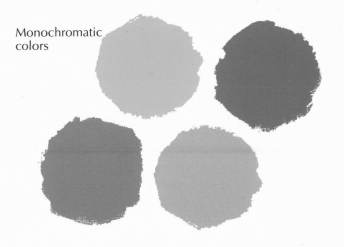

Complementary color

Positive space—The area of a design in which objects are drawn or painted.

Sans serifs—Letters that do not have extra lines at the top and bottom.

Serifs—Lines added to the top and bottom of letters for interest or beauty.

Shadowing letters—Extra lines along one side of a letter to give it dimension or depth.

Shine lines—Strong highlights along the edge of objects to simulate light striking the edge.

Sideload—A brush that has had paint added to one side with clean water on the other.

Sit-down shadows—Darkened areas under objects to make the objects look like they have cast shadows.

Stylus—A tool, usually wooden with a metal extension on the end that has a small ball on it, used with graphite paper to transfer patterns.

Tendrils—Small, curling shoots that grow off some vines and flowers.

Visual balance—Moving objects within a design so the positive and negative space is balanced.

Wash—Adding water or medium to a paint to make it thinner and more transparent.

Tendrils

PART 1

 Gathering Your Supplies

ABC Starting With Basic Fonts

JOK Using Your Own Handwriting

Laying Out Your Design

Transferring and Painting Lettering

GATHERING YOUR SUPPLIES

Most of the supplies you will use for handlettering are ones that you probably have around your home or workshop. They can be purchased at almost any art, graphics or office supply store. It's not necessary to purchase the brands that I use—most substitutions will do as long as you follow the guidelines I've suggested.

Tracing Paper

I learned from cartoonists to do all of my sketching or drawing on tracing paper. When you need to change a portion of a design, just place a clean piece of tracing paper over what you've already drawn, copy the part you like and delete the part you don't want to use.

Tracing paper comes in many sizes and weights, or thickness, in pads and in rolls. I like to work with a 9"×12" or 11"×14" pad of midweight paper. If you use paper that is too cheap, you'll find that it isn't very transparent and tears easily if you try to erase on it. On the other hand, vellum—a high grade of paper used by draftsmen and architects—is too expensive for drawing. Use a paper that is approximately 11 lb. and is fairly inexpensive.

BASIC SUPPLIES
From left to right: tracing paper in pads and roll, Sakura Pigma permanent black pens, rulers in several sizes, erasers and refills, graphite paper in gray and white, no. 2 pencils, double-ended stylus, paper towels, water container, assorted brushes.

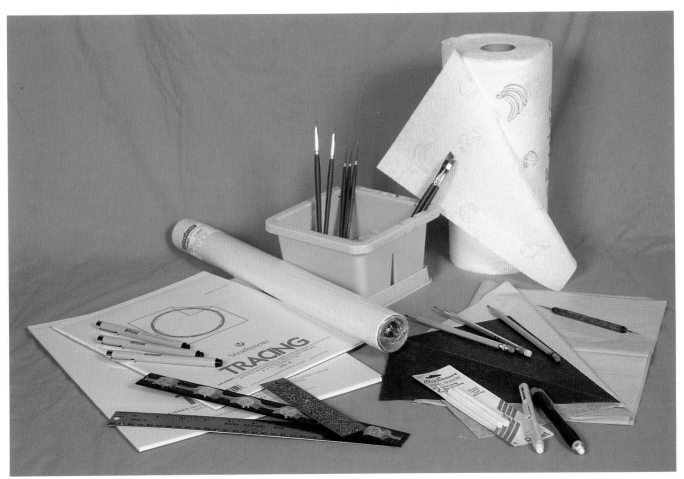

Photo by Beth O'Keefe

Pencils

No. 2 pencils are best for layout and sketching and are readily available. Softer pencils are too messy and smear, and harder ones tear the tracing paper.

For correcting the pattern before painting, use a regular lead pencil for light-colored surfaces and white charcoal pencils for dark-colored ones. (I don't recommend using pastel pencils with acrylic paints. Their binder is oil-based and can repel water-based paints.)

Erasers

I like the white, nonabrasive erasers that come in dispensers like ink pens. Several companies make them and they are available at office supply stores, drug stores and wherever ballpoint pen supplies are sold.

Pens

The Sakura Pigma permanent black pen, size .005, seems to work best for me. Other fine-point pens work as well as long as the ink is permanent, not just waterproof. Refillable pens work well too, but remember to clean them before you put them away.

Rulers

Metal rulers with cork glued to the back are best for inking. They come in many lengths, from six inches to twenty-four inches long. If you do not have one with cork backing, use any other ruler and first tape several pennies to the back to keep from smearing the ink when you move the ruler.

Graphite Paper (Gray and White)

This is probably the most difficult item to find. It must be greaseless, but sensitive enough to transfer without heavy pressure. Most good art supply stores sell sheets or rolls of greaseless graphite in both colors.

Some artists like to make their own graphite paper by rubbing a soft black pencil over the back of their tracing if they are transferring onto a light-colored surface, or white chalk for a dark-colored surface. This is too messy and time-consuming for me, but it will work.

Never use typewriter carbon paper. You won't be able to get it off your painting surface.

Stylus

It's very important to have a stylus with a fine point. Most come with two tips on opposite ends, one fine and one heavy. Since most lettering is rather small, it's important to use the finest end to transfer the design to the painting surface. Using a pencil or other blunt point can give you wide, messy lines that will distort the shape of the letters when you are ready to paint them.

Paper Towels

Any commercial roll of paper towels will do; the more absorbent, the better.

Water Container

To protect your brushes and insure that you have removed the paint from them, it is best to have a commercial brush basin. These come in several configurations, but a good one will have ridges on the bottom that you can push and pull the brush over in a painting motion to agitate the bristles and allow the used paint to flow out into the water. A divider in the middle to separate clean water from dirty water is a good feature, too.

Paints

I prefer to work with water-based, bottled acrylic paints. They dry fast, are easy to clean up and come in so many colors that it is rarely necessary to mix additional colors. Be sure to choose a brand that has sufficient pigment to cover in one coat when basecoating and one where the pigment doesn't separate from the binder too quickly. A smooth, creamy texture will make painting easier because the paint will flow off the brush more efficiently. Be careful not to use bottled acrylics that are classified for craft projects. They are very low in pigment and not suitable for this type of painting. (Remember, you get what you pay for, so check the prices. Paints that are cheap usually have less pigment.) Tube acrylics are rich in pigment but are too thick for stroke work and need to be thinned down with medium to flow smoothly from the brush. Be careful not to mix gouache, a water-based paint with a different chemical binder, with acrylic paints. They are not compatible. Oil paints can also be used, but they too must be thinned down with medium and take a long time to dry between base coat and embellishments.

Brushes

Because you will be working with water-based acrylic paints, I recommend using Golden Taklon synthetic brushes. I have found that natural hair brushes get "fat" when filled with water and do not work as well as the Taklon brushes.

For basecoating letters with wide "legs," use a flat, a one-stroke or filbert brush the approximate width of the leg. For thin lettering and details or fine lines, I recommend a short liner, a no. 0 in most cases. For very fine lines or tiny lettering, I use a no. 000 short liner. Any brush smaller than a no. 000 will not hold enough paint and will need to be refilled constantly. Long liners or "scrollers" can be used if you are an experienced painter with strong skills in brush control.

For floating colors and general painting, I recommend the angle brushes. Their sharp points side-loaded with color fit so well into those tiny little triangular spots where shadows start.

When purchasing brushes, be sure to check that all of the bristles are straight and smooth with no permanent bends or curves. The flat, filbert and one-stroke brushes should come to a good chisel edge and the liners should have very sharp points. Quality brushes are an investment, so chose carefully and keep them clean and in good condition.

So many projects have been ruined by painters using old, worn-out brushes to execute fine detail work. When the brushes no longer have sharp points and clean edges, give them a decent retirement and use them for basecoating or craft work. Always check your brushes before you begin painting to be sure they are clean and in good condition. Rinse them out well to remove any cleaner before you start painting. Never stand them on their bristles or leave them soaking in water containers.

Brushes photographed by John Murphy, Cocoa Beach, Florida.

ONE-STROKE BRUSHES

One-stroke brushes look like flat brushes, but the bristles are much longer. They come in limited sizes and range from 1/8-inch to about 1-inch wide. They are excellent for basecoating work because they hold more paint in their extra-long bristles, making it unnecessary to reload the brush as often as with shorter flat brushes. They, too, should have sharp chisel edges and no stray hairs sticking out.

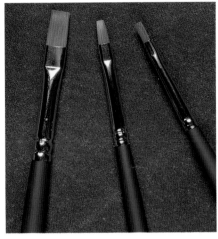

FLAT BRUSHES

Flat brushes come in a large range of sizes, from very tiny no. 0 to large, wide no. 20 or larger. The bristles are molded flat by the flattening of the metal ferrule. All of the bristles should come to a sharp chisel edge when the brush is wet, with no stray hairs sticking out from the ferrule. They are used for basecoating as well as floating color.

FILBERT BRUSHES

Filbert brushes also have a flattened ferrule, but the bristles are arranged to form a soft oval at the tip, earning them the name "cats' tongues." They are excellent for basecoating letters, especially those that turn and have many soft edges and points. Good brushes will have a smooth transition of bristles across the oval and will form an oval point when dampened.

SHORT LINER BRUSHES

Short liner brushes should have no stray hairs sticking out from the ferrule and should come to a sharp point when wet. Do not purchase brushes that are blunt or have been bent in shipping. Great care should be taken when storing these brushes to be sure that they are protected during movement. Because of the few bristles in these brushes, they won't last very long and should be checked for wear before use.

ANGLE BRUSHES

Angle brushes are shaped like flats, but the bristles form a sharp angle across the chisel surface. They can be used for basecoating letters that have many sharp notches and angles and for side-loading floated color across the legs of letters. By loading the sharp point of the angle and floating the color toward the short side, angle brushes can easily fit those tiny triangular areas where shadows often start.

STARTING WITH BASIC FONTS

Most of the lettering we will use in this book can be broken down into three kinds of fonts: Roman, script and text. These fonts frequently overlap and can be called many other names, but for our purposes we'll classify them this way.

Much of the personalization and handlettering we do is with a basic Roman font. It is easier to read and copy, and lends itself to more ways of shaping and stretching it. The examples of Roman fonts on pages 15, 16 and 17 show some of the many ways the basic Roman alphabet can be used.

Script fonts are loosely based on early examples of Spencerian handwriting and can be very feminine and flowery, with added scrolls and frills. Many people still hire professional calligraphers to pen elaborate invitations and notes using the Spencerian script. There has been a recent resurgence of interest in learning this beautiful way to write, and calligraphy classes can often be found in craft shops and schools. Examples of script fonts are shown on pages 18, 19 and 20.

Text fonts are much more difficult to read and paint but are wonderful to use for initials in personalization and for very formal writing on documents like diplomas and awards certificates. They are usually written straight up and down, perpendicular to the line with very rigid rules about the distances between each letter. Some examples of text fonts can be seen on pages 21, 22 and 23.

ROMAN

This is a basic Roman font.

Script

This Spencerian script was defined by Platt R. Spencer, called the "man who taught America how to write," around the late nineteenth and early twentieth century. He set a style and standard for penmanship, strictly adhered to by industry and business, which clarified bookkeeping and provided a beautiful form for personal correspondence. In later years, this very formal style was replaced in schools by the Palmer method of penmanship.

This text font is called English Gothic. It is a refinement of handwritten manuscripts dating back to the twelfth century. Since most people could not read or write at that time, this writing was largely restricted to royalty or religious congregations.

ABCDEFG
HIJKLMN
OPQRSTU
VWXYZ

abcdefgh
ijklmnop
qrstuvw
xyz

ROMAN

By shadowing these Roman alphabet letters on the right side and putting lines in the center of the letters, you can create the illusion of dimension to an otherwise flat letter.

ABCDEFG
HIJKLM
NOPQRST
UVWXYZ
abcdefg
hijklmn
opqrstu
vwxyz

A B C D E F G
H I J K L M N
O P Q R S T U
V W X Y Z
abcdefghijkl
mnopqrstuvw
xyz
1234567890

Spencer's flowing lines were made with an offset pen point that was only pulled downward and never pushed upward, creating the thick and thin legs of the letters. As the penman became more secure in his craft, extra flourishes and frills were added.

Handlettering for Decorative Artists

$$A\ B\ C\ D\ E\ F$$

$$G\ H\ I\ J\ K\ L$$

$$M\ N\ O\ P\ Q\ R$$

$$S\ T\ U\ V\ W$$

$$X\ Y\ Z$$

SCRIPT

This more angular script font still follows the form of the earlier fonts but is broader and more stylized.

A B C D E F G
H I J K L M
N O P Q R S
T U V W X Y Z

a b c d e f g h i j k l
m n o p q r s t u v
w x y z

Handlettering for Decorative Artists

Later refinements made this English Gothic alphabet easier to read, although it still required great skill and patience to copy.

A B C D E F
G H I J K L
M N O P Q
R S T U V W
X Y Z

a b c d e f g h i j
k l m n o p q r s
t u v w x y z
1 2 3 4 5 6 7 8 9 0

Handlettering for Decorative Artists

This modern version of a text alphabet is much more streamlined but is still reminiscent of the flat, squared-off penmanship produced by wide, flat pen points.

ABCDEFGHIJKLMN
OPQQRSTUVWXYZ

abcdefghiijjklmno
pqrrrastuvwxyz

USING YOUR OWN HANDWRITING

There are many times that we want to personalize things, especially gifts for friends and relatives on special occasions like births, weddings and graduations. Personalized gifts seem to be kept longer and please the recipient the most. Photo albums, storage boxes and momentos for weddings and births are just a few of the gifts that can be easily personalized.

For a simple method of personalization, use your own handwriting, based on the old Palmer penmanship taught in many schools. You may remember the written alphabet above the blackboard in the front of the room, and spending hours of practice making round, flowing, ''slinky'' ovals. Each loop and flourish had to match the one before it.

There are pads of paper available at art supply and drafting stores with the lines already printed in light blue (the blue will not reproduce on a copier), which give you a ready-made practice pad to work on. In fact, I found some really inexpensive ones in the school supply department for elementary students.

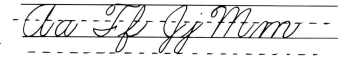

The Palmer method starts with two parallel lines with dotted lines in between and below them. The ascenders have to touch the line above, all of the lowercase letters have to touch the dotted line in the middle and the descenders have to touch the dotted lines below.

All of the letters have to be on the same slant.

This exercise helps you evaluate how far you've come in adapting your handwriting to your personality from those early school days.

Never try to write or paint directly onto the surface you have prepared without making an accurate tracing first. I guarantee something will not work out and you will end up like the famous sign below. It only takes a few extra minutes to work it out on tracing paper and then transfer it with graphite to your surface. Your results will look much more professional.

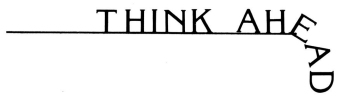

Painting a Straight Design

If you want to personalize or put a name on something that is on a straight line on a flat surface, make an alphabet the correct size, on a copier or by hand, then trace the letters of the alphabet onto a straight line on your tracing paper and transfer the letters to the surface you have prepared. By using the tracing paper, you can see the surface underneath and center the lettering.

Painting a Curving Design

If you are planning on personalizing a banner, ribbon or any object that curves or bends, first transfer the outline of the object to a piece of tracing paper. By marking the center where you want the lettering to be, you establish a starting point for counting backward and forward so the word is centered. By using the tracing paper to work out your design, you are able to shift the pattern slightly if needed to accommodate the difference in the size or shape of different letters. When working on a curved surface, like the banner I used, it isn't always possible to just copy lettering. Sometimes it is necessary to print it in freehand; a little time and patience will give you an excellent result. By blocking in the shape and size of each letter as a guide with a piece of tracing paper, you can fill in the details of different fonts for each letter later on.

1 Decide how far from the edge you want your lettering to be and make parallel lines on the tracing paper into which the top and bottom of the lettering will fit.

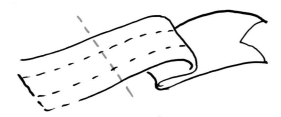

2 Mark where you want the center of the lettering to be with a vertical dotted line.

3 Count the number of letters you will be using and start the middle letter or space over the vertical line.

4 Work backward from the center line to the beginning of the word.

5 Work forward from the center line to the end of the word.

6 After you remove the pattern and ink the lettering, you'll have a professionally finished project that you will be proud to share.

◄ *Remember that the letters should be perpendicular to the guidelines and not lean over. All of the letters should touch the top and bottom guidelines for visual accuracy.*

◄ *Most of the letters in an alphabet should have "legs" the same width. Usually, crossbars on letters like A and H will cross at the same place.*

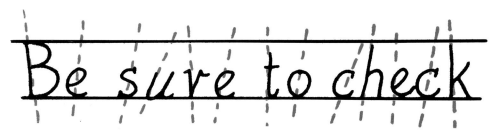

The biggest mistake painters make when they use lettering is not getting the letters even. Our eyes and brains have registered all forms of graphic lettering all of our lives. When we see lettering that is not perpendicular to the line or slanting in different directions, we instinctively know it's wrong, but not always why it's wrong.

LAYING OUT YOUR DESIGN

I am not a symmetrical person. By that I don't mean that my eyes are crooked on my face or one shoulder is higher than the other. What I mean is that I am not comfortable with things that line up perfectly on a wall or are mirror images of each other. I have been known to rearrange objects that are too neatly lined up and bump gently against pictures that are too straight. My husband, on the other hand, is a symmetrical person. He will get out the tape measure and measure from the floor to the ceiling to hang pictures just so on a wall.

Making Thumbnail Sketches

When talking about layout with lettering, you must first decide if you want a design that is symmetrical or asymmetrical. The easiest way to decide that is with *thumbnail sketches.* These are quick little sketches of all of the material you want to include in your design. By spending a few minutes sketching alternative ways to create balance in your work, you can decide which part is most important and which part should dominate the design.

As an artist, the most important elements of most designs are usually the objects in the design. By using blocks of space for each part, you can see if the positive elements of the design (the parts that are filled with things) are balanced with the negative space in the design (the areas that have nothing in them). A design can become too crowded by using too many elements. One of the ways to avoid overcrowding is to allow one element to dominate the design while others become smaller or less significant.

In a design that has only lettering in it, as in a poster or banner, you must decide which words are most important and then list the other wording in descending order of importance.

BOY SCOUTS OF AMERICA   12-4 P.M. SAT., NOV 21ST

CENTRAL FLORIDA NEIGHBORHOOD FOOD DRIVE

1 Write down or sketch all of the information you want included in your design, including any artwork.

 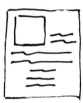

2 Make as many thumbnail sketches as needed until you work out a layout that pleases you.

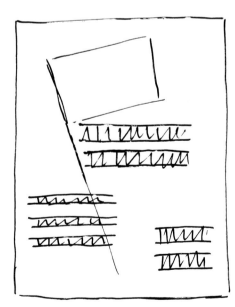

3 By deciding on the most important information you want to put in your layout, you can determine the relative size of each group of words.

4 The finished design has been worked out in a thumbnail sketch, and you are now ready to make an enlarged version to fit the surface.

Choosing a Font

When a layout has been worked out that pleases you, it is time to consider the size of the area you will be working with and decide upon a suitable font or fonts to use. The message you want to convey will usually dictate the type of font to choose. Some fonts are feminine, some are masculine and some evoke certain moods or eras. If the design will be used in an area where it needs to be read quickly, ease of recognition is important and will probably rule out fancy script and text fonts. Simple, clean, bold Roman fonts usually fill the bill.

Art Deco fonts are reminiscent of the twenties or thirties, and complement bright, bouncy designs.

This script font is usually considered very feminine and lends itself to designs especially for women or turn-of-the-century Victorian pieces.

Images of the Wild West when "men were men" are evoked by this very masculine font.

Deciding on Colors

Color is an important factor in creating your design and helps to create a mood or attract attention. Colors that are soft and pastel remind us of spring; colors that are bright and clear remind us of summer; colors that are strong and neutral evoke thoughts of fall; and cool or monochromatic colors remind us of winter. Strong contrasts in colors draw attention more quickly. When choosing colors for your design, keep these guidelines in mind, as well as the area the design will be used in and, most importantly, what pleases you.

The pastel colors of spring are wonderful for designs incorporating children and pets, and make us feel soft and cozy.

Strong, vivid, neutralized colors bring memories of turning leaves and goldenrod.

Clear, bright colors feel warm, like the summer sun.

The cool blues and grays of snow and winter skies, with hints of bare ground and leafless trees, echo the cold of winter.

Strong contrasts of colors attract attention more quickly and draw the eye.

Making a Final Sketch

When all of these elements have been decided, it is time to make a final, finished sketch of the design that is full size and covers the area you will be working on. Block in the lettering in each shape or section of the design and then either hand copy the details of a particular font, or enlarge or reduce fonts on a copy machine until they can be traced to fit. As mentioned earlier, I recommend using tracing paper for drawing. It is then a simple step to pull a clean piece of paper over the sketches and make a final drawing that is ready to be traced onto your surface.

Using Optical Spacing

Now that you are ready to fill in the exact size of each letter, it is important to say a few words about the spacing between letters. Because each font has letters of different widths, depending on their shape and size, it is far easier to lay out a design with optical spacing. The shape of each letter in most fonts helps to determine how close it should be to the next letter. Some of the letters in Roman alphabets are a normal width, like *E, B, C, D, G, H, K, N, O, Q, R, S, U, V, X* and *Z*. Others are narrow, like *F, I, J, L, P, T* And *Y*. And some are wide, like *A, W* and *M*. Some letters are round and others are tall or thin.

Your eyes are your best reference when working with spacing. The amount of space taken up by each letter makes it difficult to use a mechanical means of laying out Roman letters with a ruler. You will notice in the middle illustration, which has been mechanically spaced, that the striped bars that indicate the spaces between letters are all the same width and carefully separate each letter with identical spaces. No part of the letters overlap into the space. This clearly illustrates how stiff the word looks with this type of spacing.

The optical spacing of the bottom example shows how much more pleasing it is to the eye when you take into consideration the shape of each letter, and nest the letters together by overlapping into the space in between each letter when necessary. You still need to work to keep the same *area* between each letter without causing the letters in the word to look too squeezed together or too far apart. Optical spacing creates a visual balance that your eyes and brain have been trained to recognize from all of the lettering you have seen and stored in your memory.

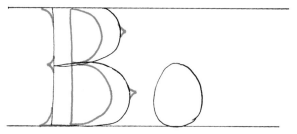

First fill in the simple block lettering between the lines (the part done in black), then go back and add the dimensions and details of each letter (the part done in red).

The spacing for this word is done with mechanical spacing, measuring the exact distance between each letter with no consideration for the shape of the letters and allowing no overlapping into its neighbor's space.

The spacing for this word is done with optical spacing, still making the area between each letter the same width, but taking into consideration the size and shape of each letter.

Handlettering for Decorative Artists

Some of the more formal fonts, especially text fonts, have rigid rules about each letter being the same size and occupying the same space; a form of mechanical spacing is automatically imposed when you use them. Most of the script alphabets have letters that overlap and invade the space of other letters for flow and beauty, so optical spacing is necessary when working with these. The rule of thumb is to go with what looks best.

The swirls and flourishes of the script alphabet allow us to nest the letters together as long as the slant of each letter is the same.

Most text letters have identical spaces between them and look better with mechanical spacing.

Spacing Exercise

For a fun exercise, cut out the letters of a font alphabet and try arranging them next to each other to see how the different letters lend themselves to nesting against each other.

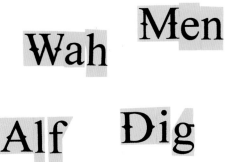

TRANSFERRING AND PAINTING LETTERING

After you have worked out your design on paper, make a finished drawing with a fine-point pen on tracing paper. This will be your pattern.

Make sure the surface you are working on is properly prepared. If the surface is painted, spray it first with Krylon no. 1311 matte acrylic spray to seal the paints and make a smoother surface that will not "grab" the pen.

Check to be sure the pattern is correctly placed on the surface and carefully tape down one side of the tracing paper. If necessary, cut the tracing paper with the design on it to fit the surface, especially on surfaces that are round or curved. Slip the appropriate white or gray graphite paper under the tracing and hold it in place while carefully drawing over the design with the fine end of the stylus. Transfer only the most necessary lines that you will need to paint with.

Do not transfer the pattern directly to your surface from the original drawing. The pressure required to transfer a design from regular copy paper through graphite is too strong and can leave indentations on the surface that may be hard to remove later.

Check to make sure you have transferred all of the necessary details you will need to paint the design and that all of the lines are correct and straight. Lay the original drawing next to your prepared surface and look for any blanks or mistakes on the copy.

Checking for Accuracy

When a design is transferred to a surface by using tracing paper, it often becomes distorted. The paper might slip, the design might have been copied incorrectly to the tracing paper, the pen or stylus used to transfer it might be too wide, you might not have steady hands, the phone may ring and distract you in the middle of the transfer—a thousand things can happen to move or

Drawing two parallel lines at the top and bottom of each word gives you a guide for checking to see if the pattern has been transferred correctly. Look for ascenders to touch the top line and be sure all of the letters sit on the bottom line. The letters should all be on the same slant or perpendicular to the lines.

This is an example of how easily the paper can slip or move during transferring. It would be best to erase or remove this and pattern it again.

The pattern on this tracing is slightly distorted, but can be easily corrected during painting.

By painting slightly beyond where the traced pattern is (the area in red), the design was corrected without having to remove the graphite pattern.

distort the lines. Checking for accuracy before painting gives you the option of correcting mistakes with your brush without having to erase and repattern.

Before painting your lettering, use a ruler and sharp pencil—lead for light surfaces and white charcoal for dark ones—and check to see that all of the letters line up from top and bottom. By drawing faint parallel lines along the top and bottom of each row of letters, you can see if the eye will accept the painted design as straight and even. If there is a great discrepancy, remove the pattern and transfer it again.

If possible, when the discrepancy is slight, it is easier to correct by overpainting the letters. Too often when the graphite pattern is removed by an eraser, the graphite doesn't come off completely, and you wind up with a smeary mess on the prepared surface. You can often correct slight deviations by painting a hair beyond the graphite lines to make the letters a little taller, coming up to the line; a little shorter, staying in the lines; or a little thicker or thinner.

Remember to remove all graphite lines as soon as the first application of paint has dried. When graphite has been captured under paint or varnish, it is often there forever, so erase guidance lines as soon as they are no longer needed. Repaint any areas where the paint may have lifted during the erasure.

Finding a Brush

The first step in painting lettering is to find a flat, angle, filbert or one-stroke brush the approximate width of the legs of the letters you are working with. Finding a brush that is good for painting lettering is very important. In the section on supplies, I suggested Golden Taklon synthetic brushes for use with acrylic paints. Experiment with different brands until you find the one that lasts the longest for the way you paint. If you work in oils, watercolors or gouache, use good quality brushes designed for those mediums.

The letters on this tracing did not quite reach the top lines, but were easily corrected during painting.

The first letters of the two words were above the line and were easily reduced during the painting.

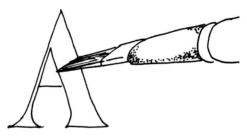

Lay the flat brush against the lettering to see if it will fill the whole leg of the letter during painting.

Filling in the Letters

Thin down the paint with water or medium to make the paint flow off the brush smoothly. Think of lettering as a form of stroke work, for which you thin most paints to the consistency of India ink.

Predampen several letters at a time—the larger the letters, the less you should dampen at a time. Fill the brush with paint and place the chisel edge of the brush at the top of a leg of a letter and pull down, filling in the whole leg with paint in one stroke. By predampening the surface, the paint will flow on more smoothly, there will be no stop and start lines from dried paint, and no ridges will build up along the edges from heavy paint.

If necessary, you can go back later and fill in any little notches or lines with paint on a smaller flat brush or liner; however, painting or touching up wide legs of letters with a liner or round brush will make your lettering look streaked and uneven, so use the largest flat brush you can for any given area. Very small lettering or script can be filled in with a liner. Be sure to use a brush large enough to fill in the legs of the letters with one stroke.

When all of the lettering is filled in, go back and evaluate the paint coverage. Because the surface was predampened before painting, the first application may be thin and transparent. If you want darker, more opaque lettering, dampen again and follow the same steps. Remember that it is much better to start with a lighter coating of paint. You can always add more color, but it is difficult to remove a color that has become too strong.

Cleaning Up the Edges

To clean up the edges of the lettering, outline the outside with either a contrasting color or black. Don't be afraid to use an ink pen if your skills are not good enough with a fine liner. Just remember to clean up lines of graphite before varnishing. If you use a permanent ink pen, spray the surface first with a light coat of Krylon no. 1311 matte acrylic spray to seal the paints and protect the pen from picking up paint and clogging the point. Keep these lines fine and straight. If you make a mistake, just use the background color to clean up around the letters. When the base coats are dry, details and embellishments can be added.

The small corners of the letter (areas in the dotted circles) were filled in with a liner brush after the original base coat was painted in with a flat brush.

The letter on the left has only one thin coat of transparent paint. The second letter has an additional layer of paint for heavier coverage.

This progression of painting steps demonstrates how strength of color and details are added. The first letter has only a thin, transparent layer of paint. The second letter has a heavier additional layer of paint, and the third letter has been outlined and detailed to add interest.

Outlining or Shadowing

Outlining or shadowing around lettering should usually be done with the liner or a very small flat or filbert brush. Shadowing around the letters gives them dimension and adds dramatic emphasis to a word. It makes the letters stand out and helps draw the eye to that word or phrase. The shadowing can be added to either side of the letters, but should be consistent throughout the word. You are creating the illusion of depth, so the principles of perspective apply, with the shadows being on either the left or right side of all of the parts of the letter. This can usually be done freehand if you are comfortable with drawing from perspective, but if it is a new theory to you, it is best to lightly pencil in the lines before painting them. Many fonts come with built-in shadowing, which will help you to understand the technique. See page 49 for instructions on shadowing letters from different perspectives.

The first letter has been outlined with a black permanent pen. The second letter has been shadowed on the right side.

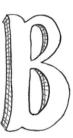

The first letter has been shadowed on the left side, as though the observer is standing to the right of and below the letter. The middle letter is shadowed to suggest the observer is standing in front of but slightly to the right of and on the same level with the letter. The third example has the observer standing to the left of and above the letter.

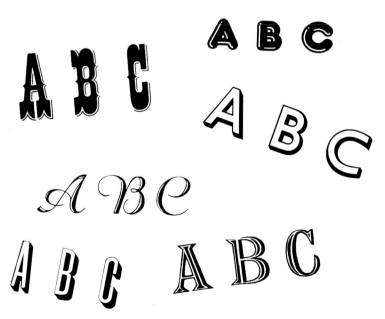

These examples of letters with shadowing demonstrate the drama and interest created when shadowing is painted around the letters.

PART 2

ROMAN FONTS

WORKING WITH COMPUTER FONTS

The most versatile fonts are the Roman fonts; they are easily read and provide a good foundation for creative changes. By adding lines at the bottom or top of the letter (called *serifs*), a more formal letter is created. Perhaps those of you who use a computer or have worked in calligraphy will recognize the term *italic* for slanting a letter to the side to create a new look for a font. Letters that are elongated and made taller are called *condensed* and add a grace and elegance to some projects. They also work well in small, narrow spaces where you have a lot of lettering to insert. A font that is stretched from side to side is called *extended*.

All of the font changes at right can be made on your computer. Below is a good example of ways the computer font Mature can be modified electronically to give different looks to the same basic letters. If you know people who are comfortable working with a computer, by all means ask them to print alphabets for you in various fonts in at least 48 point. (*Point* refers to the size of the letters in the font.) They will probably be delighted to help you, and you will have a great reference for designing projects. In fact, I found that my children and grandchildren love to show me how clever they are with the computer and are anxious to help out a novice.

On the next few pages I have given you examples of ten Roman fonts. Most of these fonts were provided by the Expert Software company on their CD "2000 Fantastic Fonts." Notice the similarities in the general shapes of the letters, but also notice the differences in them. The most noticeable differences are in the legs of the *W*, the tail on the *Q* and the length of the *J*.

The basic letter A *from a simple Roman font.*

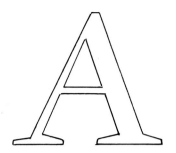

Lines added to the tops or bottoms of letters in an alphabet are called serifs. *Letters without lines at the top or bottom are then referred to as* sans serif, *or without serifs.*

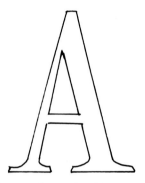

Stretching or elongating letters vertically is referred to as condensed *lettering. This also makes them narrower so that more letters will fit into a space. These letters can also be slanted to make them italic.*

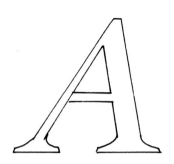

This letter A *has been slanted to the side and is referred to as* italic. *The degree of slant is determined by the writer, but all of the letters in that word or font must be on the same angle or slant.*

MATURE FONT

MATURE ITALIC FONT

MATURE CONDENSED FONT

MATURE CONDENSED ITALIC

MATURE EXTENDED FONT

MATURE EXTENDED ITALIC FONT

© 1994-1997, Expert Software, Inc.

ROMAN

A B C D E F G H I
J K L M N O P Q R
S T U V W X Y Z

a b c d e f g h i j k l
m n o p q r s t u v w
x y z

1234567890

A B C D E F G H
I J K L M N O P
Q R S T U V W X
Y Z

a b c d e f g h i j
k l m n o p q r s
t u v w x y z

1234567890

A B C D E F G H I J K L M N O P Q R S T U V W X Y Z

a b c d e f g h i j k l m n o p q r s t u v w x y z

1234567890

Century font
© 1994-1997, Expert Software, Inc.

A B C D E F G H I
J K L M N O P Q R
S T U V W X Y Z

a b c d e f g h i j k l
m n o p q r s t u v
w x y z

1234567890

A B C D E F G H I J K L M N O P Q R S T U V W X Y Z

a b c d e f g h i j k l m n o p q r s t u v w x y z

1234567890

A B C D E F G H I J K L M N O P Q R S T U V W X Y Z

a b c d e f g h i j k l m n o p q r s t u v w x y z

1234567890

A B C D E F G H I
J K L M N O P Q
R S T U V W
X Y Z

a b c d e f g h i j
k l m n o p q r s t
u v w x y z

1234567890

A B C D E F G H I J
K L M N O P Q R S
T U V W X Y Z

a b c d e f g h i j k l
m n o p q r s t u v
w x y z

1234567890

ROMAN

A B C D E F G H I J K L M N O P Q R S T U V W X Y Z

a b c d e f g h i j k l m n o p q r s t u v w x y z

1234567890

Handlettering for Decorative Artists

A B C D E F G H I
J K L M N O P Q R
S T U V W X Y Z

a b c d e f g h i j k l
m n o p q r s t u v w
x y z

1234567890

ADAPTING COMPUTER FONTS

Computer fonts offer an endless variety of lettering styles to choose from, but you aren't limited to just what you can produce on a computer. Computer fonts are simply a foundation for your creativity. Once you've chosen a font, you can adapt it by hand, adding decorative elements that make it your own. For example, by adding a block at the top and bottom of each leg, a new font is created that has a western or masculine look to it. By drawing curving flairs at the top and bottom of each leg of a letter, a more formal font is created that gives a feminine look to the letters. Little notches on the sides of each leg are very formal and create an Old World feel. Points or arrowheads at the top and bottom of each leg makes me think of Ivanhoe and Robin Hood.

All of these changes and moods have been created from the basic Mature font. If you add just these changes to the other ten Roman fonts shown, think of all the possibilities you will have.

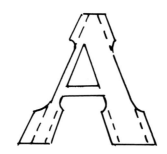

By laying tracing paper over the top of a letter, you can draw the changes you want to make. Be sure the size of the blocks at the top and bottom of each letter are the same size. It helps to make an accuracy line along the top and bottom surfaces of the blocks before transferring it to a surface to be painted. I see this font as very masculine and often use it in projects for men and boys. Its formal font name is Stagecoach.

Serifs at the top and bottom and notches along the side that extend to the left and right from the main legs of a letter create a totally different look. Remember to place the notches in approximately the same place on each letter, using an accuracy line if necessary.

The addition of curving flairs at the top and bottom of each of the legs of a letter gives a flow and softness to the letters. Be sure to allow enough room between the letters to add the flairs or the letters will overlap each other. When changing to this look, remember to curve the tops of E and F as they extend to the right.

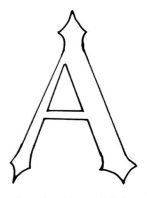

Another font that has a definite masculine flair is created by adding points or arrowheads to the tops and bottoms of each leg. This would look especially attractive on lettering that has been condensed to make it taller.

CREATING DEPTH

If you want to create more interest or drama once you have blocked in your letters, consider *shadowing* them. By this I mean to create a shadow line along the legs of the letters that makes the letters look three-dimensional. This is done by applying the simple rules of perspective and vanishing points. To understand these rules, study the illustration at top right: A simple diagram of two-point perspective (you can see the vanishing point on both sides of you) shows that you are standing, not lying down, on the ground in front of the object. Therefore, the vanishing points are above ground level. You are slightly to the left of the objects, so you see the left sides. As with the telephone poles on the right, you can still see to the right, so the objects disappear that way. Every line that flows to the left or right (the dotted lines) is on the same line flowing toward the vanishing point, depending on which side of the object it's on. Therefore, the tops of the windows are on a common line and the tops and bottoms of the telephone poles are stretched to the same vanishing point. Also notice that as the telephone poles progress away from you, they become shorter, narrower and closer together. The rules are the same for lettering.

The following examples show a letter with different perspectives or viewing angles. If you imagine you are standing to the left, right or below the letter, you can see the sides or depth of each letter. (The perspective from above the lettering is very confusing to read and I do not recommend it for most designs.)

Simple perspective

Vanishing point

Vanishing point

Vanishing point

Vanishing point

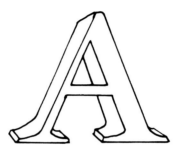

You are looking at this letter from the left side, so the shadowing is on the left side. Notice that the top and bottom of the shadowing taper to a vanishing point that is approximately in the center of the letter, not below or above it.

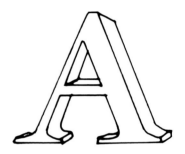

The observer of this letter is standing to the right of the letter, so the shadowing is on the right. Notice that all of the parts of the letter should be examined for shadowing, even the serifs at the top and bottom.

In this example, the observer is looking above his head for the shadowing on this letter. He is slightly to the right and below, creating shadowing underneath all of the surfaces.

ADDING SELECTIVE FLOURISHES

Of course, you are not locked-in to making every letter in a word or design exactly the same. Adding flourishes to any of the letters changes the entire look of the letter, especially the first or last letters of a word, or when there is a hole or space in the design you would like to fill. The same creative stretching can be done to any of the letters, especially in long words with similar beginning and ending letters. Probably the most fun is to nest the letters around each other to make them fit a space and still be readable. All of these ideas are only the beginning of the many fun ways a basic Roman font can be changed and altered.

By extending the bottom of this letter S and curving it around itself, a decorative flourish is added to the letter.

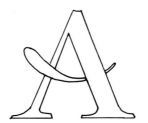

This A has a carefree, happy look because the crossbar in the center has been curved up and around the legs of the letter. This flourish could be extended by curving the line over the top of the letter on either side.

The right leg of the letter R has been dramatically extended below the line and curved up under the next letter. This same technique can be used on other letters, like A, C, E and L, and the tails of Q, R and Z. This sometimes helps to draw the word together and create unity.

Stretching the beginning and ending letters on this word helps hold the letters together and draw interest. Notice the flourishes for added zest on the right leg of the Rs.

Probably the hardest but most rewarding way to manipulate letters is to nest them into a preformed shape and still be able to read them. This took a lot of time and experimentation but is my favorite challenge of all the lettering I have done. In this example, it was necessary to shorten some of the letters, like the N, to get them all to fit. You will not be able to work with a preprinted alphabet for this, and it does require a basic understanding of the shape of each letter in a particular font. The finished design is shown at right.

Antiques and Collectables Sign, from the book *Personal Collection* by Jackie O'Keefe; photographed by John Murphy, Cocoa Beach, Florida.

PATRIOTIC LETTERING

On the following pages, I share some step-by-step designs using Roman fonts to help you learn to create and design your own projects with lettering.

UNCLE

1 Use a standard font to shape the letters (the basic Mature font was used here), being careful to keep the width of each leg the same size and all of the letters perpendicular to the line. The notches on each side of the main legs add detail and a place for the horizontal dividing line between the two painted areas. Check your spacing before transferring a finished design to be sure it is accurate and pleasing to the eye. Trace the finished design to the surface with graphite and a stylus.

UNCLE

2 A line at the top and bottom of the letters gives a check for visual accuracy before painting the base coat of Blueberry Blue acrylic paint on the top half of each letter. The bottom half is the background color of Snow White. With a fine liner, make Napa Red vertical lines equidistant on the bottom of each leg.

UNCLE

3 Erase all of the graphite lines and outline around the letters with Ebony Black on a fine liner, or, if you prefer, outline with a fine-point black permanent pen. Paint a division line of Snow White horizontally across the center of each letter at the notches. I recommend making little dots with a white charcoal pencil for the placement of the stars. These do not have to be exact stars, but can just be dots if the lettering is very small. It is more attractive if the stars line up straight on each leg and with each other across all of the letters. The stars are painted with white and usually require two coats of paint to cover.

UNCLE

4 Shadowing is painted on the right side with Ebony Black on a liner brush to give the impression of depth and dimension to the letters. This shadow would also be attractive with gold paint and a black outline.

Uncle Sam's Flour Recipe Box, pattern packet by Jackie O'Keefe; photographed by John Murphy, Cocoa Beach, Florida.

CREATING LETTERS THAT LOOK LIKE BRASS

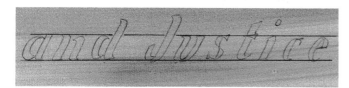

1 The phrase ". . . and justice for all," is from the Pledge of Allegiance. In this illustration, I want the letters, which are italic, to look like brass that has been attached to the background surface at the bottom. The first step is to transfer the pattern for the lettering to the surface with tracing paper and graphite. Check for accuracy by making two parallel lines with white graphite at the top and bottom of the letters. Since there are only two letters with ascenders, make the top line align with the top of the lowercase letters.

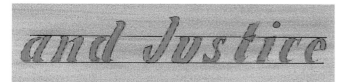

2 With a flat, filbert or one-stroke brush that is the width of the legs of the letter, basecoat all of the letters with True Ochre acrylic, painting up to and down to the accuracy lines and filling in each letter completely. Fill in a few of the finer lines with a liner brush and True Ochre. If necessary, basecoat more than once to be sure of good coverage for later shading.

3 After the base coat has dried thoroughly, sideload a small angle or flat brush with Burnt Sienna and float a shade of color across the bottom and top of each leg of each letter. I customarily dampen each area where I am floating color to keep the color soft and to avoid hard sideload lines. It may take more than one application of paint to achieve good shading, so be sure to allow the area to dry completely between each layer of paint. Dampen around the bottom half of each of the letters and float a sideload of Burnt Sienna around the outside of the bottom of each letter for cast shadows (sit-down shadows) and to help create the illusion that the lettering is attached to the surface.

4 When the paint has dried completely, deepen the shadows at the bottom of each leg of each letter and also darken the cast shadows with a mix of Burnt Sienna and Burnt Umber to help "anchor" the letters to the surface.

5 When the paint has dried completely, gently erase the graphite lines with a soft white eraser before they are captured forever in the paint. (More experienced painters may be able to erase the graphite lines after the first base coat of color.) Clean the brush thoroughly and float a sideload of Buttermilk across the middle light section of each letter, using a "back-to-back" sideload on a dampened surface. Only highlight where the base coat area is showing, never over an area where shading has already been painted in. Highlights need to be built slowly in painting, so the next application of this light color will cover a smaller area than the first and should be applied on a dry surface so the paint will not soften and diffuse. Use a liner brush and Snow White, and make little lines of sparkle and shine at the highest curve of each leg of each letter. When the highlight is acceptable, make a mix of Burnt Sienna and Burnt Umber (1:1) and, with a fine liner, outline all of the letters.

6 Check for good contrast in the shading and highlights on the letters and repeat any step needed to make the letters look like shiny metal. With a sideload of Burnt Umber, darken the sit-down shadows under the letters as needed to create an illusion that pushes the letters away from the background. The finished lettering should look as though each letter curves up in the center and shines, and is attached to the surface at the bottom of each leg.

Justice for All Desk Box, pattern packet by Jackie O'Keefe; photographed by John Murphy, Cocoa Beach, Florida.

SHADED LETTERING

1 The lettering in the word *vegetables* is a condensed or lengthened version of a basic Roman font. A dotted line is used as a guide for adding notches to the sides of most of the legs so that the notches are all on the same plane or level. Transfer the lettering to the surface with graphite and a stylus. With a ruler, make accuracy lines at the tops and bottoms of the letters and along the notches.

2 Using a flat or one-stroke brush that is the approximate width of the legs of the letters, basecoat the letters with True Ochre acrylic. Use a liner brush in tight corners or extensions. It will help to dampen a few letters at a time to allow the paint to flow on smoothly and to avoid stop-and-start marks when you refill your brush. Keep the acrylic paint thinned down with water to get a smoother flow from the brush. It is better to use multiple coats of thinned paint to basecoat than to risk a thick buildup of paint with ridges.

3 Sideload a flat or angle brush with Burnt Orange and carefully float across the bottom of each letter. Repeat this step as needed to achieve a smooth and even coverage. When dry, use a fine liner brush and carefully outline the letters with Burnt Orange.

4 With a fine liner brush and Burnt Orange, make horizontal lines across the legs of each letter, starting at the bottom and stopping about halfway up the leg, or about where the notches are. These lines should be equidistant. Clean the liner brush. With the highlight color, start at the top of each letter and make equidistant lines down from the top of each letter, ending halfway down the letter. These lines create drama and emphasize the illusion of highlight and shading.

The lettering in the word choice *is a reversed version of the vegetables lettering. The letters were traced and painted in the same manner, but the floated Burnt Orange shading was moved to the top of each letter and the highlight to the bottom.*

ILLUMINATED LETTERING

We have preserved writings from as early as the twelfth century that contain wonderful illuminated letters. Most of these were from religious orders and scribes whose only work was to record and copy the writings of scholars and royalty. Early manuscripts and books were carefully copied word for word; the only personalization allowed was the elaborate and beautiful illumination of the first letter of paragraphs or pages.

In these examples, I used the letter *P* to share some simple forms of embellishment reminiscent of those used by early calligraphers. You can use these to add flair and interest to your lettering. You will note that embellishments can be added to the inside of the letter, to the area around the outside of the letter or both. The only rule is to be sure the letter is still readable after the additions are made.

Transfer the outline of the letter (in this case, a Roman letter P with serifs and notches) to the surface with graphite and a stylus, and use a pale wash of Grey Sky acrylic paint to basecoat the whole letter. When this base coat is dry, the center section of the letter is basecoated with French Grey Blue (a middle value) in one of the two methods shown. Stay just inside the edges of the sides of the letter, leaving a pale band of the first wash showing all the way around the center section. Both examples are outlined with a liner brush and Payne's Grey, a darker value of the same color.

In the next four examples, the letters are further embellished on the insides of the legs. For a pretty, feminine look, a fine liner brush and Grey Sky are used to paint little curving tendrils with tiny flowers and leaves made of ovals and dots.

In this letter, the ovals inside the center section are basecoated with the darkest value grey, Payne's Grey, and then outlined with Snow White. The flowers inside the ovals are made with Snow White and a larger liner brush.

Here the crosshatching inside the ovals is made by using Snow White on a very fine liner brush and making diagonal lines equidistant down through the oval. When these lines dry, cross them with lines running at a 90 degree angle. Place Snow White ovals at the juncture of the lines, making sure they line up down the center of the base oval, except on curving legs like the right leg of the P. These junctions will follow the curve of the leg.

Outline around the ovals with Payne's Grey. Make Snow White dots in the center of each leg. While the dots are still wet, use a liner brush to pull lines up and down from the dots to make the lines or arrows inside the ovals.

On the next three letters, the embellishments are outside the letter P. In this example, a soft sideload of the base coat color is used to shade along the outside edges of the letter, giving it a rounded shape. Vines are then painted weaving in and out of the letter, using a color that complements the letter. Contrasting flowers and leaves are painted with a liner brush, then little dots are interspersed through the vines and leaves to help to soften the massiveness of the letter.

This type of embellishment is pretty as a personalization on stationery or a gift. The letter is first transferred to the surface and the frame drawn around it, leaving room for the scrolls and dots. Ovals, rectangles and many other shapes can also be used. Strong contrasting colors should be used so that the letter shows up well inside the box after painting. The lines and scrolls can be as elaborate as you care to make them, sometimes employing flowers, birds and even people in the area around the letter.

In this final letter P, flowers with buds and stems are painted in front of the letter, weaving through the open areas and overlapping the legs. This would be especially attractive to use with familiar flowers whose names start with that particular letter, for example, pansies for P.

EMBELLISHING WHOLE WORDS

Simple embellishments can add charm and elegance to whole words as well. This project is a good demonstration of the way a whole word can be embellished for added beauty and charm.

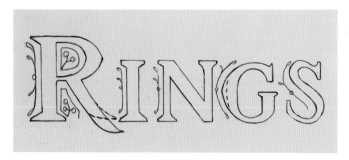

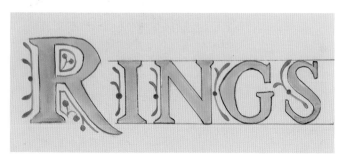

1 This lettering is copied from the Mature font with just a few changes. (The dotted lines show where the original font lines were drawn.) For drama, the right leg of the *R* is extended below the line and the left leg of the *G* is thickened a bit at the center to match the curve of the letter *S* for later linework. When transferring this design to a surface, it would be wise to leave out the lines for the embellishments and to do them freehand after the word has been painted.

2 The letters are then basecoated using a one-stroke or flat brush with a very pale wash of Antique Green. The base coat should be very pale and smooth. Any lines or small places that cannot be filled in with a flat or one-stroke brush can be filled with a liner. Just be sure to keep the paint thinned down the same amount as the previous base coat. The little decorative embellishments in front of each letter and inside the *R* are painted after the word is finished, using a fine liner brush and a mix of Antique Green and Red Violet (1:1). The dots in the linework in front of each letter are made with the same mix using the handle end of the brush. The dots for the flowers are made in the same way using Red-Violet. Be sure to allow these to dry thoroughly or you may smear your work.

3 When basecoating with a pale wash of color, it is recommended that the shading be done with the same color or a mix made of that color. Mix the Antique Green with Red Violet, its complementary color, to create a neutral green-brown for shading. (Using a bottled brown would create a look too intense for the softness required for this design.) All of the letters in the word are shaded with a float of the Antique Green and Red-Violet mix, shading along the sides of all of the legs of the letters. When this dries, outline each of the letters with the mix using a fine liner brush. This creates a look of roundness in the letters, leaving the first base coat as the highlight area.

Rings Tray, pattern packet by Jackie O'Keefe; photographed by John Murphy, Cocoa Beach, Florida.

ADDING HIGHLIGHTS TO CREATE ROUNDNESS

1 The same effect is used on this letter *A* as was used in the previous example. The letter is first basecoated with an opaque coverage of Blue Green acrylic paint. It will probably take several coats of this color to achieve an opaque coverage. Be sure to keep the paint thinned down to avoid the side ridges in the paint that will interfere with floating a sideloaded color later.

2 By highlighting along the side of each piece of the letter, a rounded effect is created. Be consistent on the side of the legs with the highlights or the illusion of roundness will not be believable. With a part that curves, like the crossbar on this *A,* either side will work as long as the highlight continues on the same side for the rest of the pieces of the letter. Although this seems like a reversal of the rings project, it is actually the same effect using highlighting instead of shading to create an illusion of dimension and roundness.

3 Adding shine lines with a liner brush of a lighter color over the top of the highlights creates further roundness and interest to the letter. The shine lines should center over the top or highest part of the rounded areas. First, make the long lines down the top of the curve; when those dry, repeat the same color with slightly wider ovals, dots or lines of sparkle.

CREATING DEPTH IN FLAT LETTERS

1 Dimension can also be created with shading and highlighting on letters that look flat. Even with these few letters, it is still necessary to use accuracy lines when painting the base coats. Erase any graphite or white charcoal lines as soon as the paint dries to avoid trapping them under areas that are painted later. After these letters are basecoated in an opaque coverage of Victorian Blue acrylic paint, they are shadowed with Payne's Grey. This creates the illusion that the letters have thickness or depth. Because the perspective is from the front and slightly to the left, all of the shadowing is on the left side. The dotted lines are then added with a white charcoal pencil just inside the edge of each of the letters to act as guidelines for shading.

2 By floating a darker shading color just inside the outer edge of the center of each letter, depth is created on the face, resembling a carved-out letter. Repeat the shading with the same color inside the letters as often as needed to achieve a smooth coverage and contour. We can create the illusion that these letters have indentations in them by remembering that, to push things away, it is necessary to darken them, and to bring things forward, it is necessary to lighten them.

3 Further highlights along the outside edges and on the shadowing emphasize the edges of the letters, while the dots and lines on the center of each leg draw the eye and create interest. Use a fine liner brush and a lighter shade of blue like Ice Blue to highlight along the edge of the letters on the left side of each leg. The lines and dots inside the center sections of each letter are made with Snow White. Make the lines first and then use the handle of the brush to make the dots. Remember, dots take much longer to dry, so wait before handling again.

Gran's Toys Box, pattern packet by Jackie
O'Keefe; photographed by Greg Albert.

PAINTING ON A DARK BACKGROUND

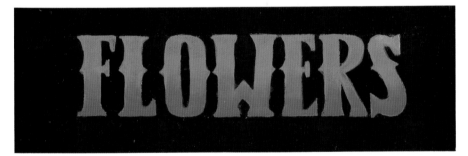

1 All of the previous letters have been painted on a light background. For extra zing, try painting on a dark background! The strong contrast between light and dark colors creates great lettering. Be sure that you have enough of the background color left for cleanup work later. Transfer the letters to the dark background with white graphite using a white charcoal pencil and ruler to mark the upper and lower accuracy lines.

2 Basecoat in the letters with a flat or one-stroke brush and True Ochre acrylic. The first three letters have been given two coats of True Ochre while the last four have only one coat of paint to demonstrate how many more coats of paint are required to cover the dark background. This particular project would probably require three coats for smooth, even coverage.

3 After erasing the white lines, the bottom of each letter is shaded with a float of Burnt Sienna to add weight.

4 The top of each letter is then highlighted with a float of Buttermilk, and Buttermilk accent lines are placed along the left side of each leg of the letters to create a look of dimension. Cleanup on a dark background is wonderful. Just use the background color to line around the outside of each letter to straighten and sharpen it.

Vickers Seedsman Chest of Drawers, from the book *Personal Collection* by Jackie O'Keefe; photographed by John Murphy, Cocoa Beach, Florida.

ADDING INTEREST TO LETTERING-ONLY DESIGNS

1   When lettering is the only factor in the design, it is necessary to make the lettering as interesting as possible. The word *congratulations* has many attention-grabbing details: It is curved, following along a free-form line; the *S* at the end was given a "tail" that underlines the word, nearly connecting with the exaggerated tail on the *C*; also, a different form of *G* that drops below the line was used to complete the enclosure of the word. The miniscule letters of the word also get smaller as they progress toward the end of the word, and the letters are nestled closer together than normal. All of these things break the rules we normally apply to lettering, but anything goes in the creative process.

2   The first step, as always, is to transfer the design to the surface with tracing paper and graphite. Check to be sure that all of the letters are perpendicular to and standing on the curving line.

3   When it's time to decide on a color scheme for a design, too often we get locked into only one way to use that design. It's a good idea to keep an open mind and experiment with different ways to present a project. The idea for this design came from a photo I had of a spectacular fireworks display. I wanted the challenge of trying to capture fireworks in the night sky.

By basecoating the whole design in a pale yellow, Taffy Cream, a base is formed on the dark background to support another brighter color. When the bright copper metallic paint is then layered over the pale yellow, a shiny look is given to the design and the illusion of exploding fireworks is suggested. With a flat brush the width of each leg of the letters, fill in the letters with Taffy Cream acrylic paint. Change to a small, short liner brush and paint the explosion marks around the center of each explosion with the same pale yellow. Dots are made in the center of the explosion with the handle of a small brush. With a small round or large liner brush, make the comma strokes for the rockets with the pale yellow. Use at least two coats of paint for good coverage.

4 Polished Copper metallic paint is added over the top of the letters, just in from the edge. Let the metallic paint dry thoroughly and outline each letter with the pale yellow to cleanup the edges. The metallic paint is also added to the bursts of fireworks to add sparkle and depth.

I used the exact same design on a white background for a graduation gift and achieved a totally different look. By using bright, happy colors, the message is still the same but the project looks totally different.

Painting Light Over Dark

The letters below show the difference between basecoating directly onto a dark background with a light color (right) and basecoating with an undercoat of light paint (middle). With acrylic paints, the dark background color is going to show through unless you use several layers of paint, so if you want strong, vibrant colors, it is sometimes necessary to first fill in the letters with a white or off-white layer of paint. The same yellow on the dark background without the light first layer could take three or four coats of paint before a similiar coverage is achieved.

Undercoat Basecoat with   Basecoat with-
           undercoat   out undercoat

French   Summer   Violet   Royal   French
Mauve   Lilac   Haze   Purple   Light
                                    Blue

Blue   Midnite   Shale   Camel
Green   Green   Green   Yellow

To paint lettering with variegated colors, first chose the colors to create the mood you want. Here I wanted many colors to fade into each other. Many shades of one color may also be chosen. When you've decided how many colors you want, decide how much space you have for each color and divide the word into areas. Lay out the colors in the right order on your palette and, working quickly on a predampened surface, fill in the letters. Where possible, overlap colors to help them blend together. When dry, outline the letters with the appropriate color.

Congratulations Tray, pattern packet by Jackie O'Keefe; photography by John Murphy, Cocoa Beach, Florida.

PART 3

SCRIPT
FONTS

THE SPENCERIAN SCRIPT

Near the end of the nineteenth century, the industrial revolution around the world forced businesses to develop a uniform method of writing. The sheer volume of paperwork in communicating with other businesses mandated the formation of business schools where bookkeeping and penmanship were taught. The average man did not read or write very well, and the educated, wealthy man did not "dirty his hands" with the everyday affairs of his business.

Apprenticeships had been the usual form of training, but involved long years of study at starvation wages. The lack of uniformity from business to business paved the way for schools that specialized in standardized forms of business management and clerking. From these schools a standard of writing emerged, filled with enough flourishes and furbelows to warm the hearts of any Victorian man or woman.

Without a doubt, the leader in this writing-style revolution was Platt R. Spencer, the "man who taught America how to write." He developed the Spencerian script, which served as a model for three generations of penmen.

These modified Spencerian alphabets are penned with an offset point in a pen stock so that the hand can be held in a normal way while the tip of the pen can be pressed and lifted to create the thick and thin lines of the letter. By pressing down and applying pressure on the downward strokes, and lifting up onto the point on the upward strokes, a smooth, flowing letter is created that can easily be modified or added to as the whim moves the penman.

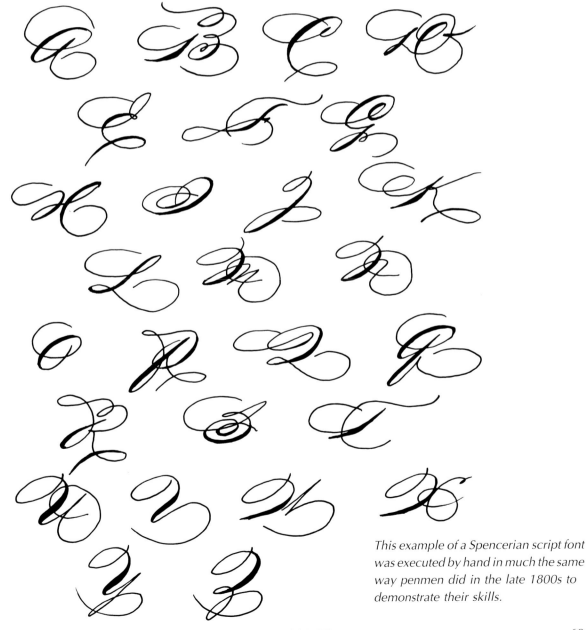

This example of a Spencerian script font was executed by hand in much the same way penmen did in the late 1800s to demonstrate their skills.

This example is also a handlettered reproduction of an even more elaborate form of the Spencerian script. Note the different interpretations of some of the letters as each penman developed his own style of flourish and scroll.

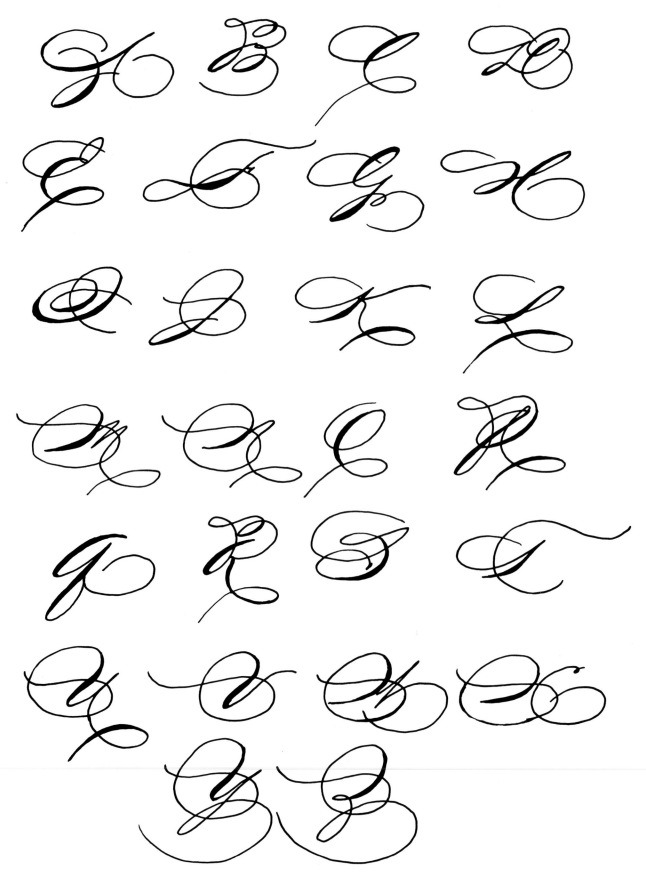

Handlettering for Decorative Artists

THE PALMER METHOD

As more children were sent to schools and a simplified method of writing was needed, the Palmer method was adopted and is still used today. By eliminating the beautiful scrolls and flourishes, Palmer was able to present a clean, well-formed method of penmanship that could be easily copied and taught. Unfortunately, it is harder to read than block printing, and by far, harder to paint.

The script fonts on the next pages are simplified forms of the Spencerian and Palmer methods, with a leaning toward simplified modern brush-stroke lettering made with round or liner brushes.

I should tell you that I am not an accomplished stroke artist. Over the years, I have learned many ways to cheat to make attractive lines and strokes with brushes. Because I am not a perfectionist, I don't worry if the comma stroke on this side matches the comma stroke on that side. In fact, I don't like it if the strokes match because I am not a symmetrical person. So if you are a great stroke artist, you are probably going to love working with the script alphabets. For those of you like me, I'm glad to share the little tricks I have devised to create attractive scrolls and flourishes.

Although the mounting of the nib for this pen looks awkward, it is actually very efficient. By mounting the nib to the side and at a 45 degree angle, the penman is able to hold his hand in a natural, relaxed position with the paper at a 30 degree angle in front of him.

Photographed by John Murphy, Cocoa Beach, Florida.

The Palmer method of penmanship has been taught in schools since the early 1900s and is still the method of choice for most school districts around the world. I can remember writing rows and rows of flowing circles and loops for many long hours as the teacher walked the room and scanned each student's posture and paper placement.

SCRIPT

A B C D E F G H

I J K L M N O P

Q R S T U V W

X Y Z

a b c d e f g h i j k l m n o p

q r s t u v w x y z

A B C D E F G H

I J K L M N O P

Q R S T U V W

X Y Z

a b c d e f g h i j k l m n o p q

r s t u v w x y z

1 2 3 4 5 6 7 8 9 0

The Signet Roundhand script font can
be painted with liners or round brushes,
as can the next three fonts.

A B C D E F
G H I J K L
M N O P Q R
S T U V W
X Y Z

1 2 3 4 5 6 7 8 9 0

A B C D E F
G H I J K L
M N O P Q R
S T U V W
X Y Z
1 2 3 4 5 6 7 8 9 0

Zimmerman script font
© 1994-1997, Expert Software, Inc.

Scheherazade script font

© 1994-1997, Expert Software, Inc.

A B C D
E F G H I
J K L M
N O P Q
R S T U V
W X Y Z

1234567890

The Brush script below and the Matura font on page 80 are similar to the other script fonts, but are painted using flat or filbert brushes.

A B C D E F
G H I J K L
M N O P Q R
S T U V W
X Y Z
1 2 3 4 5 6 7 8 9 0

A B C D E F
G H I J K L
M N O P Q R
S T U V W
X Y Z

1234567890

Lowercase Letters

Not all of the fonts come with miniscules (lowercase letters), but any of those shown here will work with the other fonts. The numbers are usually interchangable too. Just be sure to choose ones that have the same character as the capitals and follow the same rules that you use for the Roman alphabets.

Script letters are usually nested a little closer together to simulate flowing handwriting, are on the same slant to the line, and have ascenders and descenders that touch the half space lines above and below. When painting these letters with a round or liner brush, concentrate on making the major lines thicker on the down strokes, just like the penman did with his pen. Keep the liner or round brush up on its tip and use paint that has been thinned to an India ink consistency.

Since these fonts are harder to read than block or Roman fonts, it is very important to keep the lines as fine and clean as possible. Sloppy or thick painting will only give you unreadable words that mar your project.

Capital Letters

The capitals are much easier to paint because they are full and spread out so beautifully. Use the proper guidelines for tracing or drawing, and be sure to check the slant. Nearly all script fonts are italic, and letters going every which way make them nearly impossible to read, much less paint.

Try to avoid a backslant as well. Western eyes have become accustomed to a right slant in their writing. Therefore, writing or printing that slants to the left will make the observer uncomfortable. This is especially true of personal handwriting. When you want to personalize a project with your own script handwriting, be especially careful to use a right-hand slant.

I tend to think of script fonts as feminine because they are so pretty. It is a great deal of fun to play with script fonts by adding extra flourishes and swirls, pulling a leg down below the line or adding extra fullness to the curls. This type of experimentation with the letterforms will give a personal touch to your lettering and help to create a specific mood with the project.

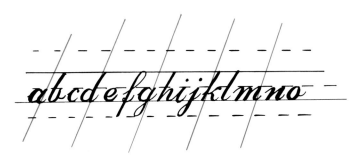

Miniscules, or lowercase letters, should always be copied onto parallel lines so that slant and spacing can be corrected at once.

It is often attractive to enlarge the first capital letter of a word or sentence. This can be done with a copier or by hand, whichever works best for you. Just be sure to check that the slant is the same as the lowercase letters and the proportion is acceptable.

By experimenting with the legs and flourishes on this letter M, a whole new look is achieved without changing the font style. Serifs can also be added to the top or bottom and the legs can be widened to create different looks and moods. Drawing the letter above or below the lines is also fun.

ADDING INTERTWINING FLOURISHES

1 This design uses three capital letters, *S*, *D* and *P*, which were personalized with flourishes and swirls for a feminine look. These letters were chosen because they stand for the Society of Decorative Painters, an international association of painters who share a love for all forms of functional art.

2 The central letter *D* was enlarged on the copy machine to about 170 percent, then traced onto tracing paper. By first tracing the *S* and *P* on the same line, it is possible to lay the larger *D* over the top and center it between them. You will note that the largest portion of the *D* extends over the top of the other letters. (Three different colors were used for the tracing to show how the letters were lined up.)

3 The three letters are then checked for slant by laying a ruler along the main legs of the letters and drawing lines through the tracing. Any errors are corrected before the letters are transferred to the painting surface. The next step is to decide which letter goes in the back or whether the letters are to be intertwined. In this project, the larger central *D* is in the back, the *S* and *P* are in the front, and none of their parts intertwine.

4 Using a no. 2 short liner brush, Summer Lilac acrylic paint is applied to the larger *D* in the center of the design. It requires two coats for opaque coverage. When this is thoroughly dry, use the same brush to paint the smaller *S* and *P* with Raspberry Acrylic paint. These are painted on top of the D.

5   With a ¼-inch angle brush sideloaded with Plum (a darker value of lilac), shade along the left side of each of the legs and scrolls of the *D*, being careful to decide which part of the flourishes are over the others, and painting on cast shadows on the parts in the back. If it is not possible to avoid the other letters, it might be wise to wait until the *D* has been shaded to paint the other letters. Repeat this procedure if needed for smooth coverage and shadow. It is attractive to have the scrolls and flourishes of each letter intertwine around itself. This is best done by floating a darker value of the color on the parts that retreat under other parts, remembering that things will appear to retreat if they are darker and come forward if they are lighter.

6   The two smaller letters are then shaded on the left side of each leg with a sideload of Raspberry on the ¼-inch angle brush or flat. In order to make them appear farther out into the light and brighter than the larger letter in the back, these two letters are highlighted with a liner brush and Snow White. Fine lines of Snow White are pulled along the right side of the legs and some of the scrolls of the letters. When this dries, small sparkle stars are painted on the fullest part of the legs, where they will shine the most.

7   After all of the letters have been completed, trace on and paint the stems and flowers. This pulls the letters together into one cohesive design and enhances the project. I used green on the tracing to show where the vines and stems intertwine with the letters—over and under themselves and in and out of the scrolls on the letters. After the paint on the letters has dried thoroughly, the tracing is laid over the design and the vines are carefully transferred onto the surface with gray graphite.

8   Paint the stems and leaves with a fine liner brush and Shale Green. With a larger liner, fill in the flowers with French Mauve. With Midnite Green sideloaded onto a ⅛-inch angle brush, shade at the base of each flower and leaf. With Raspberry sideloaded on the ⅛-inch angle brush, deepen the color of the flowers in the tiny triangle of dark where the calyxes cross on the side of each flower. Change to a fine liner brush and darken a few of the stems where they go over the top of the letters with Midnite Green. Keep this top design very light and soft so that it doesn't become more important than the letters. These additions may be as simple or complex as you desire, using the stylized types of flowers that I used, or any particular flower or vine that appeals to you. Just let your imagination fly.

SDP Bowl, pattern packet by Jackie
O'Keefe; photographed by John Murphy,
Cocoa Beach, Florida.

FLESHING OUT SCRIPT FONTS

1 Because the script fonts are harder to read, I frequently use them in conjunction with other block or Roman lettering. The phrase *For Good Girls and Boys* was designed to be secondary lettering on the lid of the toy box shown on page 62. By mixing several different fonts in one design, focal areas are established to convey a particular message. The size and dominance of the word *Toys* immediately suggests what is in the box, but further information is conveyed about who the toys are for: good girls and boys. Using the script font for this extra message gives a light, fun aspect to the message. I started by handwriting the words on three parallel lines and checking to see if the letters were on the same slant.

2 Each letter is then *fleshed out*. This presents a better guide for spacing when the letters are painted. Fleshing out means making the legs for letters look wide or thick enough to paint. Doing this before transferring the pattern to the surface gives the artist an extra aid. It provides guidelines for the brush so that the spacing between the letters can be checked ahead of time. If the design is painted without this extra step, it is too easy to get busy painting and not notice that the thickness of some of the legs of letters has caused gaps and squeezes between the letters and words.

3 The letters for this phrase are painted with Blue Green acrylic paint using a larger liner brush that fits the width of the leg. Using too fine of a brush prevents you from making the letters with one stroke of paint. Each time you need to add paint to the letter is an opportunity to make a mistake. By using a no. 1 or no. 2 short liner brush, enough paint is carried to the surface to make each leg or curve in one sweep. Hold the brush perpendicular to the surface and use the fine tip for the thinner parts, and lower the brush down to press out more paint from the side for the wider parts of the letter.

CREATING A FOCAL POINT WITH LETTERING

1 The first word for this label is written with an italic Roman font while the second two words are done with a straight script font. This is frequently done to create drama or interest in a composition or design. By using multiple fonts and slants, the project draws the reader's eye to the most important part of the work—in this case, the name of the company. This mixing of styles of letters is especially effective when designing signs that will be read quickly.

2 The same type of fleshing out used in the last example is employed on the cover of the *Heritage Farm Annual*. After first writing out the words, the letters are made thicker for ease of painting. When all of the letters have been checked for slant and accuracy, the design is then copied to a clean piece of tracing paper with a fine-point pen and transferred to the surface with gray or white graphite.

3 The large letters of *Heritage* are basecoated with a sideloaded brush of Raspberry. By floating sideloaded color down on the side of the legs of the letter, a rounded dimension is given to the letters. This is most easily done on a dampened surface, using clean water to facilitate the smooth coverage of the acrylic paint. This step can be repeated as needed to make sure all of the letters have the same uniform coverage and are the same intensity. By thinning the paint for the words *Farm Annual*, the same transparent coverage is achieved so that all of the words are the same intensity of color.

4 Notice that two different slants are used as well as two different sizes of letters. This helps to add interest and creates a focal point with the word *Heritage*. For deeper color on the large letters of the word *Heritage*, sideload a 1/4-inch angle brush with Deep Burgundy (a darker shade of red), and float another layer of color over the previous lighter color. This should cover a slightly smaller area so that the lighter color, which was applied earlier, is still seen on the left side of the letters. The words *Farm Annual* are not deepened in color so that they stay lighter and less important than the first word. All of the letters in the words are then outlined with the darker red to clean up the edges and keep the words crisp.

5 To add further drama to the words, shadow an even darker value of red, Antique Maroon, on the bottom and lower left sides with a no. 0 short liner. This step helps to create the illusion of anchoring the letters to the surface by making them look heavier on the bottom. The larger word is then highlighted with a liner brush and Buttermilk paint down the fullest part of each leg.

Heritage Farm Annual Book Cover,
pattern packet designed by Jackie
O'Keefe; photographed by John Murphy,
Cocoa Beach, Florida.

CREATING A FOCAL POINT WITH LETTERING

87

MORE EXAMPLES OF ADDED FLOURISHES

The next three examples are additional ways to add drama to lettering by adding flourishes to simple words. Only your imagination can limit the wonderful ways these script fonts can be enhanced and beautified when they are painted.

1 This is another example of fleshing out script lettering for painting. The first step is to write out the word using a simplified form of Spencerian script.

2 Next add flourishes and flairs to the letters. This could also be traced by using one of the script fonts. The red lines in this example of the capital letter *F* demonstrate how to continue existing curves into flowing scrolls and curls.

3 These are then fleshed out on the curves to give added dimension, creating a lovely, flowing word. It isn't always necessary to widen the whole leg. Sometimes you can do fanciful things like making the bottom parts of the legs wide and heavy without widening the top of the letters. Always start with at least one straight line to stand the letters on, even if you are just tracing the letters onto tracing paper. If you are using some form of hand penmanship, it is a good idea to use two or three lines to make sure all of the letters are the same height.

4 After the word is enhanced, transfer it to the surface with gray graphite.

5 Basecoat the letters with a wash of a pale blue, then shade at the bottom by floating on a darker blue-green color. Outline the whole word with a dark blue permanent pen, then shadow the letters on the left side with Glorious Gold paint on a short liner.

Handlettering for Decorative Artists

1 In this word, the capital *E* is moved in close to the small *D* to enclose the word.

2 As the scrolls and curls are fleshed out, the word is further enclosed with decoration, helping it to stand alone as an entity of its own.

3 A wash of French Mauve is first basecoated over all of the letters. After drying thoroughly, a sideload of Deep Burgundy (a darker red) is floated along some of the sides and bottoms of the letters and scrolls. All of the work is then outlined with a very fine liner brush and thinned-down Deep Burgundy paint.

An alternative way to paint this word is by basecoating only the center part of the design with the pale pink and the extra ornamentation on the top and bottom with a pale blue. The pale pink is then darkened at the top of the sections with a sideload of a darker red or burgundy color that has a blue cast to it, like Cranberry Wine or Deep Burgundy. The pale blue sections are tinted here and there with touches of the darker red color, as though the sections have reflected color from the pink areas. When you contrast the two examples, it is easy to see how multiple colors create drama in a design.

The tail ornamentation below this word is the dominating factor in this design.

This word has a lighter look than the previous one even though it has two scrolls on the tail. This is achieved by keeping the lines finer and adding more flourishes above the word for balance.

This word is fairly simple, but notice how the diamond shapes are repeated over and over for continuity in the design.

ENHANCING PROPER OR BUSINESS NAMES

1 Proper or business names in script fonts can also be greatly enhanced by creative painting. The name *Manchester* was first copied in a script font, then fleshed out. You may have noticed by now that I favor projects that look like advertisements or labels. I don't know of a fishing tackle place by the name of Manchester, although I'm sure there is one, somewhere. I am very careful never to use or duplicate any name from an actual place unless it is considered in the public domain, like the names of towns or cities.

2 After transferring the word to the surface with gray graphite, accuracy lines are added above and below the miniscules for ease in painting. A filbert brush the approximate width of the legs of the letters is loaded with thinned-down Alizarin Crimson paint to basecoat the letters.

3 Switching to an angle brush sideloaded with a very dark red that is made by mixing black with the Alizarin Crimson, shade along the bottom edge of each section of each letter, and in the curls at the bottom of the large *M*.

4 After the paint has dried and cured, outline all of the letters with a permanent black pen to keep them crisp and easy to read. This outlining can also be done with black paint on a very fine liner brush.

Manchester Fishing Tackle Box, pattern packet by Jackie O'Keefe; photographed by John Murphy, Cocoa Beach, Florida.

Handlettering for Decorative Artists

BRUSH STROKE SCRIPTS

The brush stroke scripts, Brush script and Matura MT script, are painted the same way as the Roman fonts were by using a flat or filbert brush the width of the legs of the letters. Remember to keep the paint slightly diluted and to predampen for ease of flow and smooth coverage. These scripts can also be enhanced by adding further flourishes in ways similar to the other script fonts. Just remember that these are more modern fonts and are designed to complement more up-to-date projects.

Brush stroke script fonts are probably the easiest of the script fonts to paint because all of the parts of the letter are pretty much the same width. Just re-member to hold the brush at a 45 degree angle and keep the paint thinned down with water.

This brush stroke font, Matura MT script, has more flair than the previous font but does not have a slant. That makes it a little harder to work with because the surface must be tilted to compensate for the perpendicular strokes of the brush.

PART 4

TEXT FONTS

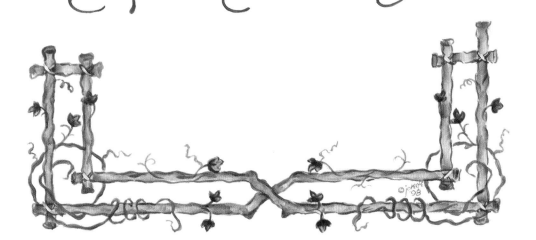

A HISTORY OF TEXT FONTS

A wise man once said, "The written word is the lifeline of civilization." Like civilization, the written word has changed and evolved over the centuries. Since the earliest days, man has recorded his thoughts and dreams, deeds and transactions in some form of writing. I would like to share with you some of the earliest forms of alphabets that I call text fonts. This covers many forms of manuscripts (alphabets handwritten by man) as well as some of the type fonts later developed from those early writings.

For our purposes, I will go back before the eighth century to the early Celtic countries, whose people developed a type of writing called uncial (shown on page 96); then on to the German monks, who developed the immensely popular Gothic Blackletter (shown on page 97); and finally to the Norman scribes, who contributed the Carolina miniscules (shown on page 98).

The Celts long preceded the Germans in the conquest of western Europe. Their sweep from the west, long before Christianity, established them in settlements across Europe as far east as Asia Minor. When the Celts embraced Christianity, the Irish monks carried the art of the book, in the form of the *Book of Kells*, to the earliest cloisters the Celts had established around their world.

Soon afterward, the Anglo-Saxon and Germanic monks took over, but their influence did not lessen the work of the previously trained scribes and artists of the orders. With the added influence of the Germans, the spread of the Gothic black letter across England and northwestern Europe in the twelfth through fifteenth centuries established a more uniform manuscript. (This form of writing was called black letter because of its dark, heavy appearance and angular shapes, caused by a wide pen being held to make a slanting stroke.) With the influence of the Norman scribes, the miniscules (lowercase letters) were added to the majuscules (capitals), and the popular form of Gothic lettering we are familiar with today was born.

Copies of the earliest alphabets are missing three of our letters: the *W, V* and *J*.

Fashions change from period to period and so, too, lettering styles. In the case of text lettering, the change was at the expense of legibility. As the text letterforms became more ornate and ornamented, they became harder to read.

This copy of a manuscript alphabet is from the fourteenth
century. It is a form that was used in Celtic countries.

ABCDE
FGHIJ
KLMNO
PQRST
UVWX
YZ

Handlettering for Decorative Artists

The capital letters, or majuscules, in this alphabet are from a manuscript found in Munich in the fourteenth century. They are an early form of Gothic Blackletter writing. Note that some of the letters we use today are missing.

TEXT

These miniscules, or lowercase letters, were added to the Gothic Blackletter manuscript on page 97 by the Norman monks in the sixteenth century.

abcdefg
hiklmnopq
rfstuvwx
nzzʒ

Handlettering for Decorative Artists

This alphabet from the Celts in the eighth century is missing some of the letters we now use. They are the K, W and Z. They have, however, given you two ways to write the I or J and two ways to write the T.

ABCDEF
GHIJLM
NOPQRS
TTUV
XS

*Two ways to write the A, D , T and Z (the upside down Q
in the last line is actually an old D) were found in Westminster
Abbey from the time of Henry III in the thirteenth century.
This alphabet is a loose form of the uncial letters with their
closed C and E, and the H and K that look like our lowercase
h and k of today.*

Handlettering for Decorative Artists

By the fourteenth century, scribes were starting to add scrolls and frills to this uncial alphabet found at the British Museum. There is still no J or W and the U looks like a V. The letters at the bottom are alternate ways to write the O and M.

ABCDE
FGHIKL
MNOPQR
STⒶTV
XYZ
OM

A HISTORY OF TEXT FONTS

The German monks' influence is seen in this copy of an alphabet used in Albrecht Dürer's Prayer Book *from the sixteenth century. There was still no I or V, but a set of lowercase letters was available.*

Handlettering for Decorative Artists

This Gothic manuscript alphabet is even more difficult to read, but has smoother transition lines with more curves. It was also from the sixteenth century, but from a different country.

Also from the sixteenth century but almost unreadable, this Gothic manuscript alphabet is a wonderful example of the Blackletter look with its heavy, dark lines. Note that there is no Q.

Handlettering for Decorative Artists

By the nineteenth century, the manuscript alphabets had been made into fonts by printers. This Dutch or German alphabet contained both upper- and lowercase letters.

A B C D E F G H I
K L M N O P Q
R S T U V W X Y Z

a b c d e f g h i j k l
m n o p q r s ſ t u v
w x y z

1 2 3 4 5 Arie 6 7 8 9 0

VICTORIAN INFLUENCES

At the turn of the nineteenth century, during Victorian times, there was a resurgence of interest in letterforms. Ornate, almost unreadable fonts were developed, combining all sorts of alphabets to achieve what the fashions of the times dictated as elegant and beautiful.

Flourishes and furbelows were added to every conceivable curve and line producing often grotesque letters. Cherubs, flowers and animals were drawn around and in between the legs of the capitals, and fonts became almost unreadable.

The German influence on lettering created this early Fraktur alphabet with alternate ways to write several of the lowercase letters. Note there is no capital I but there is a lowercase i and j.

Handlettering for Decorative Artists

A later Fraktur alphabet from around 1880, which has been simplified and beautified with scrolls and frills. This font, accredited to the German chancery, shows the Victorian influence on letters—more was always better.

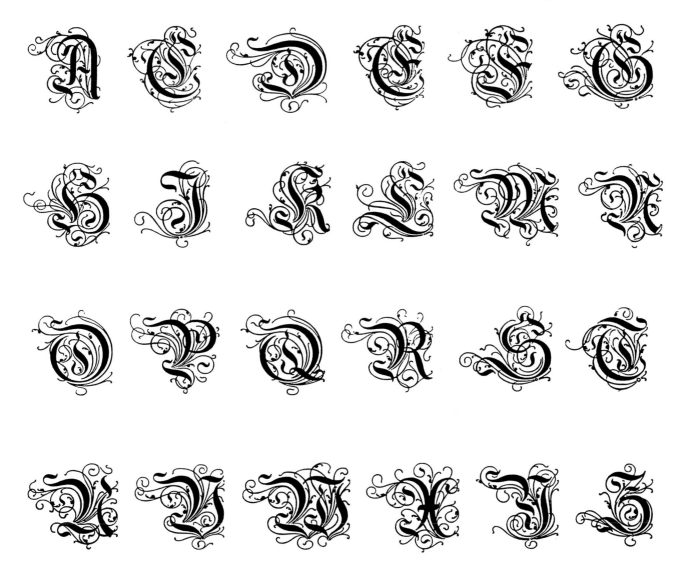

These letters were designed to be used as the first letter of the first word of a paragraph or on a page. They are an early form of mechanical illumination usually only found in work previously done by hand. As the printing press became more sophisticated, printers would commission artists to cut these intricate woodcuts for printing, replacing the work monks and scribes had painstakingly drawn by hand. Note that the letter itself is very plain and simple for easy readability.

Handlettering for Decorative Artists

The letters in this font were not so lucky, and the drawings frequently obscured the form of the letter.

Although the animals and flowers in these letters are more intricate, the letterforms themselves are very simple.

Handlettering for Decorative Artists

I'm sure some artist thought these letters were humorous with their faces and scrolls, but they are totally unreadable.

TEXT

MODERN TEXT FONTS

Over the years, our idea of beauty has changed. We have evolved to the type fonts used in computers and high-tech industries, but we haven't given up the really lovely heritage from the past.

The alphabets I offer you for working with projects using text letters is rather limited (pages 114 through 120), mainly because I don't often recommend using this form of letters. They are usually extremely hard to read, difficult to design with and exacting to paint. Like the script fonts, they have a limited application and although they are lovely to look at, they are best painted as simply as possible.

A B C D E F G H I J
K L M N O P Q R S
T U V W X Y Z

This simple Viennese font is a great example of the evolution of the Blackletter script to modern day. Clean lines with simple connectors make this alphabet easy to read and paint.

An ultramodern font with an italic slant, this Mariner font is the ultimate in contemporary letters. You can almost feel the wind blowing through your computer.

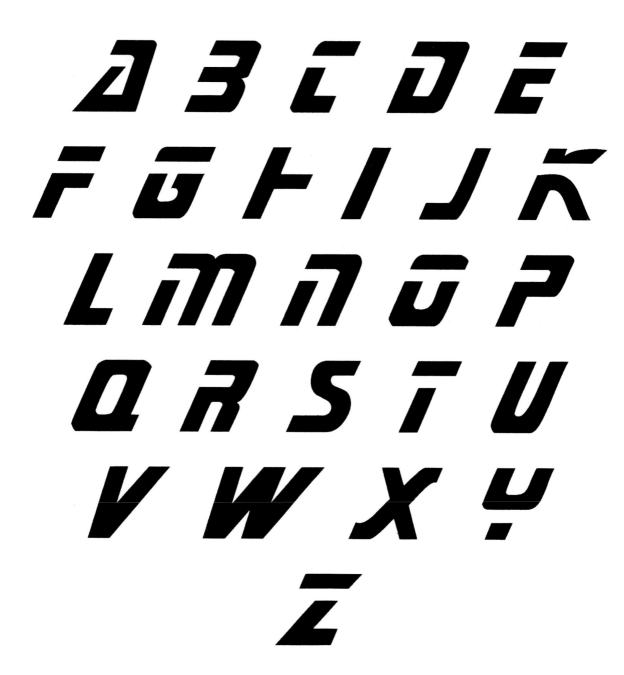

A good example of the uncial alphabet, this fifteenth-century copy from the British Museum is clean and straight.

ABCDE
FGHIK
LMNOP
QRSTU
XYZ

ABCDE
FGHIK
LMNOP
QRSTU
VUWXYZ

Handlettering for Decorative Artists

abcdefghij

klmnopqr

stuvwrxyz

1234567890

A nineteenth-century Gothic alphabet.

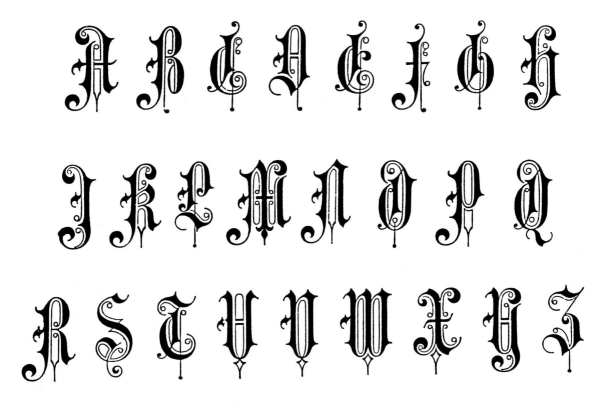

Handlettering for Decorative Artists

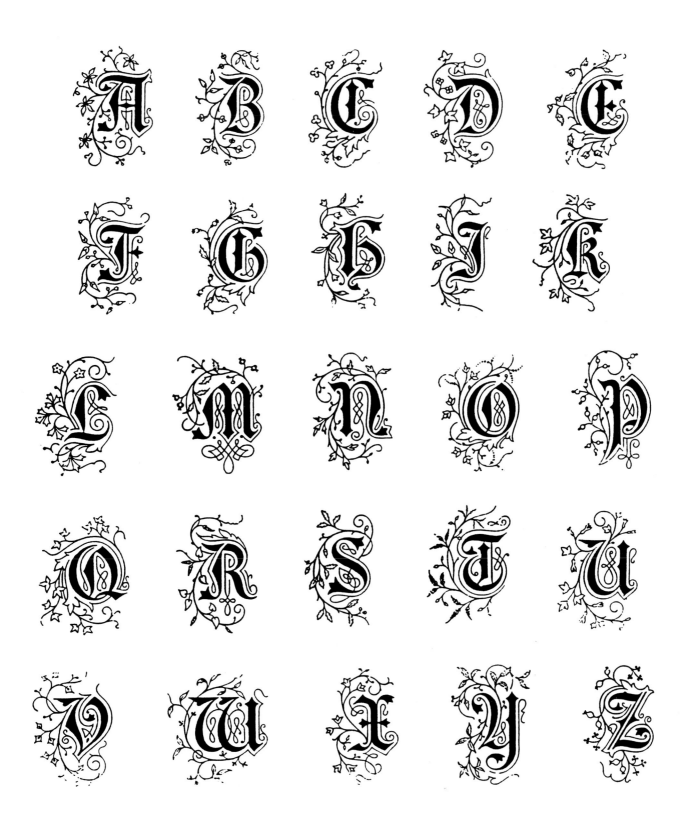

A nineteenth-century uncial alphabet with scrolls and flowers.

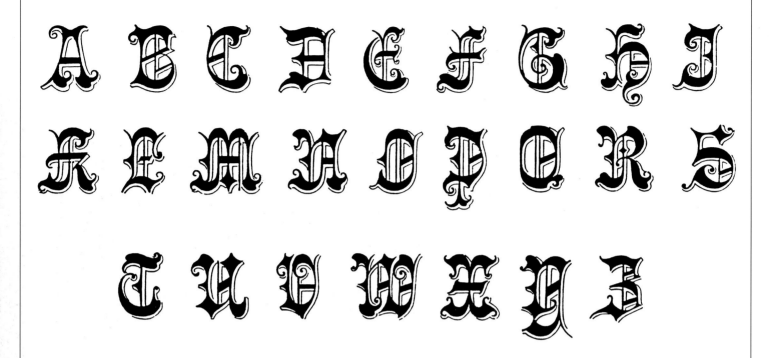

Handlettering for Decorative Artists

COLORBOOK PAINTING FOR READABILITY

When you work with text lettering, the same general rules apply that you utilized in the Roman and script fonts. Work with thumbnail sketches to determine the design placement on the surface, do your drawing and copying on tracing paper and use accuracy lines to check your tracing before painting.

For most of the fonts that I have given you, a small flat brush the width of the leg is the most efficient one to use to paint the letterforms. Hold the brush at a slight slant, usually a 45 degree angle, and pull down to make the wide part of the legs of the letter. Change to a fine liner brush and add the thin lines and connectors between the legs. If you have a very good flat brush with a fine chisel edge, some of the connector lines can be made by raising up on the edge of the brush.

1 The uncial alphabet from the opposite page is used for this project. Since this alphabet has no miniscule letters, all of the letters are capitals. They are designed on a curve to nest around the items they describe—the threads and notions. Be sure to check the tracing with accuracy lines before painting, lining up the crossbars of the letters as well as the top and bottom lines. Extra interest is added to the simple words by extending the top of the first and last letters of the word.

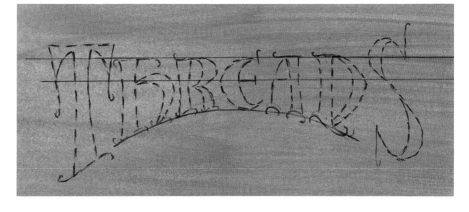

2 Because they are rather ornate, the letters are painted using a colorbook form of painting; that is, filling in between the lines with a consistent, even coat of paint. The only ornamentation is the little curves on the top and bottom lines to loosen up the massive look of the letters. This treatment makes the letters easy to read and helps draw the eye to the notions and threads that have more color and greater detail. A fine balance is then created in the design. Use a flat brush the approximate width of the legs of the letters to basecoat with Soft Black paint. Change to a fine liner brush and add lines with little curves at the top and bottom of each letter. Be sure to erase any graphite lines before varnishing. To create a feeling of oldness, a crackle background is used.

Threads and Notions Box, from the book
Personal Collection by Jackie O'Keefe;
photographed by John Murphy, Cocoa
Beach, Florida.

SIMPLE BACKGROUNDS FOR ORNATE LETTERING

1 The same treatment is used in this design, which uses the English Gothic alphabet. After tracing the letters onto tracing paper, transfer the design to the surface with graphite. The letters are then painted with Ebony Black paint using a flat brush the width of the legs held at a 45 degree slant. This fills in the letters in one coat. The word *tea* is simply painted in a colorbook manner on an oval that has been painted to look like a porcelain insert. The word is then easy to read and even recognizable from antique cannisters so familiar from bygone days.

2 A soft sideload of a medium blue paint, Uniform Blue, shades the lower side of the oval. This creates a contour to the form and suggests that this is the lower side of the oval. The shading of Soft Black around the outside of the oval is darker on the lower left side to suggest a cast shadow created by the dimension of the oval. With a liner brush, make a line around the oval, flattening the brush on the lower side for a wider line. This helps to create an additional illusion of dimension.

ADDING FEMININE TOUCHES

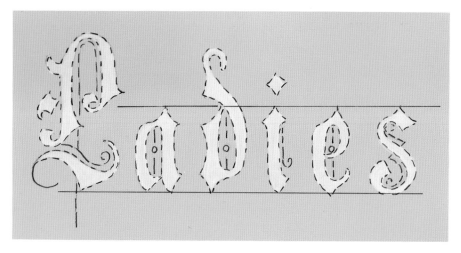

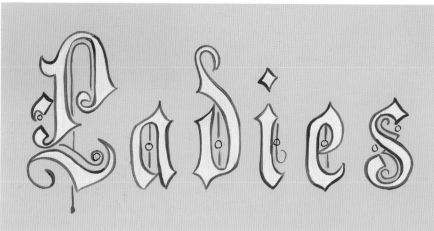

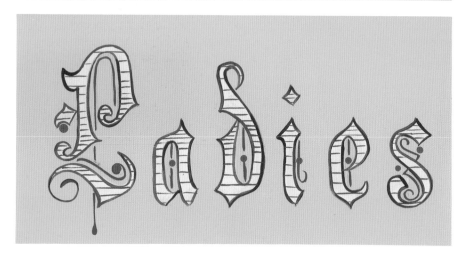

1 The same type of simple painting is also used on this ladies' room sign. The font for this project is nineteenth-century Gothic. By tracing the letters onto a guideline and enlarging the word to the proper size for the wood piece, a word is formed for a simple sign. After basecoating the wood piece with Eggshell paint, the pattern is then transferred to the surface with gray graphite. Check the word with accuracy lines to be sure the letters are perpendicular to the edges. Fill in the base coat of each letter with a flat brush loaded with Buttermilk paint, using as many coats as needed for good coverage. Be sure to erase the graphite lines.

2 Outline the letters with Antique Teal paint using a very fine liner. The decorative vertical lines outside of each letter are made with Teal Green paint, a lighter value of the color used to outline the letter.

3 With a fine liner and Teal Green paint, make the fine lines horizontally across the legs of the letters. Start in the center of each leg with the lines close together and widen the space between the lines as they progress up and down the legs. Use the tip of the handle of a small brush to make dots of Antique Mauve. The word remains readable and clear. Add extra feminine touches by painting roses and leaves around the word in coordinating colors. The roses then create a frame around the word to help draw the eyes to the focal message.

Ladies' Room Sign, photographed by Greg Albert.

TEXT INITIALS

1 It is also attractive to use a text font for initials in a design. This particular design uses a nineteenth-century font that has been given extra frills and flowers by the printer who created it. First enlarge the letter for the center of the design about 150 percent. Basecoat the background of the surface with Pink Chiffon and let it dry thoroughly. Trace the letters to tracing paper, moving the tracing paper around to create good visual spacing between the letters. Colorbook paint the letters with a flat brush and French Mocha to create an opaque coverage. Basecoat the flowers with Antique Mauve on a tiny no. 0 filbert or liner. Use a liner brush and French Mocha to paint the lines and connectors on the letters. By painting the letters in strong contrast to the background color, it is possible to immediately see them amidst all of the flowers and vines.

2 Outline the letters with Plum paint on a fine liner. The lines for the vines and stems are made with the fine liner and Shale Green paint. Shade around the center of each tiny flower with a sideload of Plum and then make the center with a dot of Plum. The leaves on the vines are made with a no. 0 filbert or liner and Antique Green. Painting the vines in a lighter value than the letters and outlining the letters with an even darker value keeps the letters as the focal point of the design.

3 Add extra detail to the letters by painting highlight lines along the left side of the legs of the letters with Pink Chiffon on a fine liner. Using a stylus, make tiny three-dot flowers throughout the design with Plum. Adding highlight lines on the letters creates even more detail and helps to maintain dominance over all of the little leaves and dots that fill in the space.

EMPHASIZING CAPITAL LETTERS

2 Outline the outside edge of the leg with the same Blue Green color, using a liner brush that is fine enough to create good, clean lines. By outlining the word, a sharp, clear image is produced that is simple to read.

1 Although the uncial alphabet does not have miniscules, it is still possible to create the look of a capital letter by enlarging the first letter of the word. The *B* of the uncial alphabet was enlarged about 150 percent to create this design. Use a bottom accuracy line to be sure all the letters are straight, then transfer the design to a surface basecoated with Blue Chiffon. With a small angle brush sideloaded with Blue Green paint, shade just inside the outside edge of the letter on all sides of the legs. This should leave a lighter center section on each leg to create the illusion of roundness.

3 Added flourishes like the cherub and flowers give the project charm and pizzazz. Just be sure to work out all of the details for additions in your original line drawing and transfer them before painting the lettering. This is not the place for freehand painting.

Conclusion

All of the suggestions for painting the letters in this book are interchangeable, and most of the added embellishments such as flowers, lines and dots will work on other alphabets. Just use your imagination and have fun adding handlettering to your painted projects.

Keep your eyes open for the wonderful vast resources that are available to you. Remember, there is nothing new under the sun; someone, somewhere, has done it before. But you can add your own special touch to the word or letter and create a gift or family heirloom to be treasured and handed down for generations.

I hope that I have given you enough information to convince you that you can use beautiful lettering in your designs, and enough inspiration to give you the courage to expand these ideas into your own unique style.